# Jumpstart Your

# Entrepreneurial

# Spirit

## Barbara J. Winter

## Foreword by Nick Williams

Sogna Bella

Sogna Bella
*an imprint of* Tethered Camel Publishing

A CIP catalogue record for this book
is available from the British Library

ISBN 1-904612-16-4

Printed and bound by Butler & Tanner Ltd.,
Burgess Hill, West Sussex UK

Tethered Camel Publishing
PO Box 12036, Bromsgrove, Worcs. UK
B60 1WT

For Dreambuilders everywhere who get up in the morning
determined to make the world a better place.
And for Zoe who reminds me why we must.

For Jacqueline,
The time to dream
bold is now!
Barbara J Winter

# Table of Contents

# Foreword

## By Nick Williams

I believe that everyone is born with at least one entrepreneurial dream. This dream is not purely selfish for personal gain alone but a dream that will be our own joy and will be a contribution to life, a dream that as we bring to fruition and live it, everyone is blessed by it. Our dreams are so precious, yet can be so vulnerable, and most of us have experienced more Dreambashers than Dream Affirmers and Dreambuilders in our life. Out of pain, disappointment or sheer lack of guidance, we often end up burying our dreams and wishing but not acting.

Jane came to me because she felt like an outsider. "Why can't I just be satisfied with a boring job like everyone else? Why do I long for inspiration, creativity, growth, joy and meaning? What's wrong with me? Why can't I be content with an ordinary life?"

As we talked it became obvious that Jane was an entrepreneur with a big spirit that she had tried to squeeze into a job. When we talked about being an entrepreneur and what her dreams were, she almost cried. "My soul felt like it had come home," she said later. I realized that the thing she thought was wrong with her was in fact her entrepreneurial spirit, a thing that was actually beautiful and precious but had never really been acknowledged. Jane never realized that she had the soul of an artist and that her business could be her canvas. Perhaps that's something you're just discovering for yourself. Or maybe you're farther along on the entrepreneurial path.

I had been an entrepreneur for over a decade when I met Barbara Winter. When Barbara came into my life four years ago she was like an old soul friend, carrying on a conversation we started some other time. She soon became so much part of my life that I couldn't believe she hadn't always been there. She is the living embodiment of the entrepreneurial spirit and my life is so much richer for her presence in it. It has also been an honor to witness her shine her light and then see lights going on, the 'aha's' and the inspiration she creates in the adult learners that we've worked with in UK, USA and Ireland.

As well as our desire to bring our dream to life, most of us need at least one major champion for us and our dreams. Let Barbara be a champion for your dreams. It's rare and wonderful to have someone who believes in us and the beauty of our dreams but it's sheer gold to have someone who also knows the how to and has the practical skills and experience to be a guide for us. It's a great gift to have someone who has pioneered ahead of us, explored the territory, made the mistakes, made the breakthroughs and now shares their wisdom. Barbara is just such a woman who's been following her own dreams for well over thirty years. She has used her life to open her heart and mind, to become a master of her craft. She is now more inspired and inspiring than ever. The Buddha said, "Your real work is to find your real work and then do it with all your heart." She is living proof of that and anyone who meets her knows that Barbara's real work is to help others find and buiid their entrepreneurial spirit.

One of Barbara's greatest gifts is of being a storyteller and each story in this book will inspire you, teach you and affirm your own entrepreneurial spirit. So read the wisdom in this book and keep your heart and mind wide open. Be educated, be inspired and informed and then do what Barbara encourages us to do—to make our life a masterpiece, a monument and manifestation of the living spirit within all of us.

God bless.

Nick Williams, London, November 2004

# Introduction

During the long years when I had the nagging suspicion that I was not anywhere close to living the life of my dreams, I had no clue that I already possessed something that would make that possible. Inevitable, in fact. This powerful force was my own entrepreneurial spirit which, happily, survived years of neglect until I was ready to recognize it and put it to work. Like others who had made the same discovery, I came to believe that this was the sleeping giant that resides in all of us. Whether or not we awaken it is completely up to us.

So what is entrepreneurial spirit anyway? I think it's more than just the catalyst for working on your own: it's an approach to life. It's living everyday with the attitude of an explorer. It's being enthusiastic about problem-solving. It's being alert to opportunity. It's an active and wildly creative way of making your own unique contribution to the world.

We see the entrepreneurial spirit in immigrant business owners and teenagers who start a rock band. We see it in mothers who invent a better baby carrier and in young adults finding new ways to use the Internet. We see it when Heifer International gives a flock of animals to a family in a Third World country. In fact, millions of people throughout the world are claiming their own entrepreneurial spirit and putting it to work every day.

Any entrepreneur soon discovers that success is truly a collection of lots of little steps and tiny bits of personal growth.

*Jumpstart Your Entrepreneurial Spirit* is also a collection of articles designed to add insight and encouragement to your journey. At the end of each article is an affirmation and a question or two for your consideration. You might answer those questions by writing them down in a journal—adding your own insights and observations.

There is simply no shortage of opportunity for innovative thinking backed up by confident action and it's my hope that this book will stimulate both. As your own entrepreneurial spirit burns brighter, you'll be inspiring and awakening other sleeping giants around you. Create. Love. Serve. The assignments don't get any better than that.

Barbara Winter
Minneapolis, Minnesota
October, 2004

# Live Long and Prosper

*My body is 56, but my soul is 17 and hungry to learn.*
Carlos Santana


Flying home from Los Angeles, I struck up a conversation with the man sitting next to me. When he told me he'd been in California on business, I asked what he did. "I have my own consulting business," he replied proudly.

"How long have you had your business?" I inquired. He looked at his watch and said, "Eight months and two weeks."

We talked a bit more and I went back to reading my magazine where I came across a series of ads proclaiming, 'Before there was the Golden Gate Bridge (Times Square, etc.), there was Brooks Brothers. Established 1818.' I smiled, thinking that in our Here Today, Gone Tomorrow culture, longevity in business is certainly cause for crowing.

Longevity was certainly not on my mind when I started my business and you may not have given it much thought, either.

Whether you want to be in business in 2020 or you have a shorter timeline, you'll build a stronger business if you consciously incorporate longevity factors into your plans.

Interestingly, many of the factors that contribute to human longevity are the very same ones that impact the life of a business.

## Practice Right Livelihood

One of the oldest longevity studies is the one Duke University has been conducting for several decades. This study focused on people who are still leading active lives after the age of 90 to find the common denominators in these dynamic elders. This study suggests that the single most important longevity factor is not whether we eat right, don't smoke or exercise (although those things count, of course). Duke says you're more apt to live a long healthy life if you spend it doing work that you love. Entrepreneurs, of course, are the ones most eager to exercise that option.

## Longevity Starts Now

Like genuine success, longevity is a cumulative process. Anne Lamott talks about that from a writer's viewpoint in *Bird by Bird*. She says, "Many non-writers assume that publication is a thunderously joyous event in the writer's life and it certainly is the biggest carrot dangling before the eyes of my students. They believe that if they themselves were to get something published their lives would change instantly, dramatically and for the better. Their self-esteem would flourish; all self-doubt would be erased like a typo... But this is not exactly what happens."

Longevity, most of the time, comes about through a relentless series of small successes, not by a single spectacular event. Kahil Gibran said, "The most solid stone in the structure is the lowest one in the foundation." How well you build the foundation will have a huge impact on your ultimate survival or demise. If your business credo is to build slow, steady, sound growth you're on your way to creating something that will last.

## Maintain a Learner's Mind

Having a successful business takes a lot more than clearing out a spare bedroom and installing a computer. Learning to think and act like an entrepreneur requires study, practice and learning over a long period of time. Without that commitment, chances of lasting success are fragile at best. "In the beginner's mind there are many possibilities," said Shunru Suzuki. "In the expert's mind there are few." When entrepreneurs stop learning, their business hits a plateau and doesn't move on.

Another longevity study is the one conducted by Dr. David Snowdon and nicknamed The Nun Study since all of his subjects came from the School Sisters of Notre Dame, an order with unusually long-livers. One of the obvious traits shared by these active older women was their devotion to continuing self-education. The most successful entrepreneurs I've met all have their personal curriculum for learning and a curiosity that they consciously keep alive.

## A Bit More From the Nuns

Two other big factors, which could not be measured but which Snowdon came to believe were significant contributors to the active long lives of the nuns, were their profound faith and their participation in a community. Snowdon suggests that spirituality gives us important tools for dealing with loss and disappointment; other longevity studies concur that the capacity to deal with loss is essential to living a long life. Ongoing interaction with like-minded people who cared about each other was integral, also, to an active life. As entrepreneurs we can and must cultivate our own spiritual gardens and find a supportive community of entrepreneurial thinkers if we're to grow a business that flourishes year after year.

So, it seems the fountain of youth has been within the reach of everyone. If you want to live long and prosper find work that you love and don't stop learning. But don't wait too long to get started. Singer Joan Baez had it right when she said, "You don't get to choose how you're going to die. Or when. You can only decide how you're going to live. Now."

*To Affirm:* I consciously cultivate a long and prosperous life for myself and my business.

*To Consider:* People who practice right livelihood, have a very different attitude towards retirement. How do you think it differs from the attitude of job-holders and why?

# The Unfailing Secret of Success
## (and other good things)

*Every calling is great when greatly pursued.*
Oliver Wendell Holmes

Shortly after my daughter Jennie graduated from college, I noticed a change in her. News that would have been greeted with an "Oh, wow!" in the past was met with a shrug or a grunt. Nothing seemed to excite her. When I mentioned my concern to my sister, she said, "I don't think you need to be worried. I was like that when I was in my twenties, trying to send the message, 'I've seen better,' so people would think I was worldly."

Happily, the enthusiastic Jennie eventually returned but not everybody passes through their blasé phase so quickly. Some people make it a lifetime policy to be unimpressed and unexcited about everything that life has to off
may think that they're displaying superior intelli
perpetually disapproving attitude, they're re
others (including customers and clients) from th
around the terminally bored is like being in a r
watt light bulbs. It's strangely uncomfortable
natural impulse to want to move into a brighter s

Enthusiasts know that apathy is an invitation t
enthusiasm is survival gear. The wise have alwa
"Success is going from failure to failure," obse
Churchill, "without a loss of enthusiasm."

## A Bit About Enthusiasm

The word "enthusiasm" comes from the Greek "entheos" which means "God within". It appears that those who are in touch with their inner spiritual fire are the most naturally enthusiastic about life itself. Of course, many people have brief moments of excitement if they make a big sale, buy a winning lottery ticket or get invited to a reception at the White House. These are temporary responses, however, and once the moment has passed, so has their enthusiasm.

Genuine enthusiasm isn't a temporary response to short-lived good fortune: it's a way of dealing with whatever life offers up. It is actually an expression of a grateful and awe-filled attitude. Most critically, it's a cultivated behavior—like good manners. The chronically cranky don't understand that they're doing it to themselves. On the other hand, the perpetually enthusiastic know that their attitude is a powerful weapon against boredom, frustration and intolerance so they take great care to protect it.

## You've Already Got It

Unlike good manners, which are totally learned behavior, enthusiasm arrives with us at birth. Watch any two-year-old exploring the world around them and you'll see wide-eyed enthusiasm in action. Unfortunately, many people believe that the role of parenting is about dampening enthusiasm, not fanning it, so too many of us arrive at adulthood with our enthusiasm dimmed and diminished. Therefore, if we are to approach our lives with enthusiasm and vigor, we need to learn how to light our own fire.

That may be easier than you think. Since enthusiasm is an innate quality residing in each of us, we can decide to release it and allow it to propel us through our lives. We can also discover for ourselves what nurtures our enthusiasm and make an effort to bring more of that into our lives. Conversely, we also need to identify those people and situations that diminish our zest and either eliminate them or find a workable way to include them with enthusiasm.

**Put It To Work**

If you begin projects with a bang but find yourself losing enthusiasm as time goes on, try going back to the beginning and remembering why you were excited to begin with. When actor Antonio Banderas was fourteen, he saw *Hair!* and decided on the spot that he wanted to act. After he finished school, he headed for Madrid and spent six months trying without success to break into theater. He returned home feeling defeated but, after three days of brooding, recalled how he had felt watching his first play. He says it made him determined to succeed and to do whatever it took, for as long as it took, to create a life as an actor. Enthusiasm can salvage all sorts of dreams that are in danger of being lost.

Speaker Karyn Ruth White, a passionate student of the therapeutic benefits of laughter, tells her audiences that when faced with a difficult situation they can get upset or they can turn it into a creative moment. Looking for such opportunities is the heart of enthusiastic living. Choosing to tackle a problem with enthusiasm is quite a different experience than suffering

19

through a challenge. The former is empowering while the latter is debilitating.

If you want to create a business that is rich, full and filled with wonder, start by releasing this magical power. Do so and you'll discover first hand what Charles Kingsley was talking about when he said, "We act as though comfort and luxury were the chief requirements of life, when all that we need to make us really happy is something to be enthusiastic about."

*To Affirm:* Enthusiasm is my natural state of being.

*To Consider:* The tiny peaceful country of Bhutan lists its top priority as maintaining its Gross National Happiness. What would it take to create a business that diligently existed to support your GNH? What would you have to banish from your kingdom? What would you have to invite in?

# Passionate Collaboration

*My knowledge of art helped me a great deal in business. The training of my eye helped me to establish higher standards of beauty and quality. Art has enriched the quality of my life by constantly leading me to the best.*
Stanley Marcus

As I watched *Winged Migration*, the breathtakingly beautiful documentary which follows migratory birds around the globe, I began to wonder what would motivate someone to spend four years filming birds in flight. I knew that the filmmakers had flown ultralight planes and devised special equipment to record the birds up close. Nevertheless, adventure needs a catalyst and I began to surmise that it wasn't a solitary passion that led to this project. Besides being passionate about the subject, it would also be necessary to be passionate about filmmaking and story-telling plus being excited to learn new things and deal with the unexpected.

## A Gathering of Passions

There's plenty of evidence to support the notion that dream-building consists of bringing together diverse passions in order to create something else and there's no better example than the original Neiman-Marcus department store.

Although Neiman-Marcus attained legendary status as a purveyor of exquisite merchandise under the leadership of

Stanley Marcus, the seeds of that mystique were sown decades earlier by his father, aunt and uncle. The elder Marcus clan envisioned a store that would specialize in selling the best and the beautiful. They thought they could do this in the unlikely and dusty cowtown that was Dallas in 1907. Nearly a century later, Neiman-Marcus remains an icon of quality and style.

There's much in the history of Neiman-Marcus that deviates from traditional business school philosophy. A reporter from *Fortune* magazine wrote this about the storekeepers in 1937:

"As for Neiman-Marcus' executives, they too live just one idea: The Store. Its madcap, or inspired, beginning sprang from an enthusiasm—an almost religious enthusiasm—that has never ceased. Herbert Marcus and his sister Carrie Neiman, and his three sons in the business, have channeled every ounce of their considerable selves into four floors of beautiful merchandise. The reason is not that they lack other interests: it would be a ghastly mistake to think of Herbert Marcus as one of those pencil-behind-the-ears Babbitts who hum brightly when they think of volume and markup and inventory; or to think of Stanley Marcus as someone who spends his evenings reading trade journals but never reading for fun. It's the other way around. They are exciting business people because in one sense they aren't business people at all; and they live the store, not by lacking outside interests, but by transferring them all inside.

"Herbert Marcus quotes Plato or Flaubert, displays a Canaletto in his dining room and dreams of owning a Renoir, but his real creative and artistic self is released in Neiman-Marcus. Similarly his sense of drama is expended there, his sense of prophecy, his powers of psychology, his strong moral sense. This moral sense runs through the whole family. It exceeds practical necessities: it isn't a matter of being 100% on the job, but rather of being dedicated to some lofty mission."

## Business is More Than Just Business

The term 'well-rounded' seems mildly old-fashioned today and schools and other institutions hardly acknowledge the possibility that individuals can function with multiple interests. As creative entrepreneurs, it's a notion we must resist and discard.

Some of the best—and certainly happiest—entrepreneurs in history have been wildly eclectic in their personal interests. Like a painter or a playwright, the creative entrepreneur gathers ideas and inspiration from many places and weaves it into the business in ways that may be subtle or obvious. Since Herbert Marcus wasn't a painter or a playwright, but a man obsessed with beauty, it's easy to imagine him challenging himself with the question, "How can I bring more beauty to the world using my gifts?" In his twenties, he'd discovered a real talent for marketing, so that gift was put to work in the service of a dream.

## The Paradox That Brings Success

I recently saw an Andy Warhol exhibit in Las Vegas and learned that his hero was Walt Disney. Why this surprising choice? Warhol said that he admired the filmmaker because he had skillfully married art and business.

Disney was not the first person to see that these two worlds could peacefully co-exist. At one time, the Venetians were the greatest businesspeople in the world. They were also passionate patrons of the arts. Dr. Albert Schweitzer was revered for his medical mission in Africa. He was equally committed to playing Bach on the organ. Mark Twain, Henry James and Robert Lewis Stevenson were not only successful authors; they were intrepid world travelers whose curiosity fed their writing. All of those creators, along with the makers of *Winged Migration* and founders of Neiman-Marcus, would surely understand what Andy Warhol meant when he observed, "After art comes business and the art of doing business is the best art of all."

*To Affirm:* My business is my apprenticeship. My big art is my life.

*To Consider:* What are the elements that collaborate in your business? What passions outside of your business influence what you create within it?

# Do Talk To Strangers

*Sometimes it's a form of love just to talk to somebody that you have nothing in common with and still be fascinated by their presence.*
David Byrne

Charles Handy cites a study by the US Center for Clinical Infant Programs which listed seven qualities children need to do well in school (and in life, adds Handy). These qualities are: confidence, curiosity, intentionality, self-control and the capacity to communicate and to cooperate. "In addition," Handy writes, "the capacity for deferred gratification turns out to be a better definition of success than IQ." If I were to draw up a list of qualities needed to succeed in self-employment, my list would be identical.

One readily available way to expand on those qualities is to adopt the program I've been advocating and call Do Talk To Strangers. Many people spend their days interacting with the same people over and over. Soon it becomes difficult to open a conversation with anyone they don't already know. It's always surprising, for instance, to watch a seminar room fill up and notice how few people greet their fellow learners. How could you not be curious about others who are about to share a learning adventure with you?

**Inspiration in Jeans**
Last year, a plumber came to make some repairs in my apartment.

As he was working on my dishwasher, I asked him if he worked exclusively for the property owner. He spun around and said, sounding insulted, "No! I own my own business." He opened his jacket and showed me his T-shirt which bore the name and logo of his company.

"So how long have you worked for yourself?" I asked. For the next several minutes, I was spellbound by his story. He had been studying veterinary medicine, Lee said, when his wife died. Since he had two young children, he found being a full-time student and caring for them too difficult so he left school.

He bought a run-down house, moved in, fixed it up and sold it for a nice profit. Then he did it again—and again. Along the way, he decided to learn about investing and put some of his profits into the stock market. His plumbing/handyman business grew alongside these other ventures. "Until two years ago, I didn't even have a listed telephone number," he laughed. "I guess I could retire but why should I? I love driving around in my truck with all my tools. And I get to learn new things all the time. You know that thing I just did to your dishwasher? I've never done that before." He was beaming as he made his confession.

That little conversation with someone who was so obviously joyful about being self-employed kept me going all day. I'm willing to bet that my genuine curiosity about Lee's life made his day better, too.

**It's More Than Just Politeness**
Learning to be comfortable in the presence of strangers has

benefits beyond merely making the day a bit more pleasant. It can have a positive impact on our mental health. Psychologist Alfred Adler observed, "It is the individual who is not interested in others who has the greatest difficulties in life and provides the greatest injuries to others."

While it's true that some of us are more naturally gregarious than others, this is an area where practice can bring noticeable improvement. Being at ease with a wide range of people is a skill worth cultivating.

**Ready, Set, Talk**
Two good starting points for opening up to strangers are:

- What is a connection that we share?

- What does this person know that I don't?

Here's how I used these two questions a year or so ago. I was connecting through the airport in Detroit and discovered that my flight to Minneapolis was delayed. I decided to find a way to make the time as fascinating as possible. I scanned the crowd in the waiting area and when I noticed a woman doing needlepoint, a personal passion of mine, I sat down beside her and asked about her needlework. After she had enthusiastically shared her project, we exchanged favorite sources for materials.

Then I asked her if she was beginning or ending her journey (a favorite conversation opener of mine when I'm traveling). She said she, too, was going home. That led to the discovery that we lived in the same part of town. But that was only the beginning. She said, "We also have a home in Alexandria." Then she added, "I grow orchids there."

Although I was the owner of one little orchid plant, I said, "I've always thought that would be a pleasant pastime. How many kinds do you have?" She really came to life as she began sharing her passion for orchids and confided that she planned to make a business out of it soon. "I understand it's quite an addiction," I joked.

"Oh, yes," she laughed. "When a plant blooms for the second time, you're hooked."

So months later when I awoke to see that the little stick in a pot in my bedroom had transformed into a blooming orchid, I knew I was a goner. I could have easily missed knowing that if I had kept to myself.

*To Affirm:* As I open myself to others, my world gets richer and fuller.

*To Consider:* What's your personal attitude about talking to strangers? Have you ever had a conversation with a stranger that led to an opportunity or idea or insight?

# Who's Watching?

*What you do when you don't have to, determines what you will be when you can no longer help it.*
Rudyard Kipling

It was one of those long travel days and I was beginning to droop. I'd spent hours flying from Zurich to Newark only to find that my flight to Minneapolis was delayed an hour. We finally boarded the plane and almost everyone was seated when a tall man appeared in the aisle next to me and indicated that he was the lucky recipient of the center seat. "I'm cranky," he said and flashed a smile. "I'm flying on a full-fare first-class ticket."

I smiled back. "Do you want to talk about it?" He shook his head and squeezed into the seat next to me. I asked if he was just beginning his trip. "No, I flew in from London," he replied.

"What were you doing in London?" I asked—thinking a conversational connection might be coming.

"I was there to do some entrepreneurial training," he replied. I may have gasped. I had found my ideal seatmate! Then he held out his hand, "By the way, I'm Dave Larue." We never stopped talking for the next two and a half hours. I learned that he'd had his own business since he was 24 (he's now 46), that he'd been doing coaching and training as a sideline for the past 10 years, that his son had started his own business. I learned a lot about the facts of Dave's life but then he told me a story that spoke loudly about who this man is.

29

**Strangers on the Plane**

Several years ago, when Dave was just starting out as a public speaker, he was on his way to Los Angeles to speak to a group of upper level managers in a company there. He planned to use his flight time to polish his talk. As the plane was boarding, he saw the flight attendant escorting an elderly man with a cane onto the plane. Dave said he was thinking, "'Please don't let him sit next to me' but, of course, that's where they put him." The 87-year-old retired farmer from North Dakota was setting off on an around-the-world journey but he was not an experienced traveler.

When the meal arrived, Dave saw the old man struggle and offered to cut up his lettuce wedge and chicken breast. Having gotten through that without incident, the man said he needed to go to the restroom. Dave walked him there and told him to just go in and not lock the door. After long minutes inside, the old man poked his head out the door and motioned to Dave. "I can't get my pants up," he said. So Dave joined him in the compartment and got him dressed. As the plane was about to land, the flight attendant came over and offered to call for a wheelchair. The man said he had his own special wheelchair with him. The flight attendant said she was sorry but their personnel were only authorized to use their own equipment. Once again, Dave came to the rescue offering to push the man in his own chair to meet the cruise representative who was meeting him. Having accomplished that, Dave left. "You know, he didn't even thank me or anything," he said.

The next day Dave conducted his seminar and talked about

attitude and the importance of treating people well. When he finished, an executive in the audience got up and said, "We hear a lot of speakers and sometimes I wonder if they really walk the talk. I'd just wanted to tell everyone here that yesterday I was sitting two rows behind you on the flight and I saw what you did for that old man."

## Character Study

When I heard Dave's story, I recalled that someone said that character is how you behave when nobody's watching. In Dave's case, it was how he behaved when he didn't know anyone was watching. Not everyone would have passed the test so well. There are many people in this world who have two very different personalities: their public and private selves. But character does not depend on outside approval; it comes from behaving with integrity in all circumstances, public or private. "Character is the total of thousands of small daily strivings to live up to the best that is in us," said Arthur G. Trudeau. "Character is the final decision to reject whatever is demeaning to oneself or to others and with confidence and honesty to choose the right." Whether anyone is watching or not.

*To Affirm:* Building character is essential to my success.

*To Consider:* Do you think building character is a hopelessly old-fashioned notion or pertinent in the world today? If character was valued, would we have had the corporate scandals of recent times? Why does character matter to a small businessowner?

# Positively Unforgettable

*We are not here to do what has already been done.*
Robert Henri

I hadn't really intended to buy a new car on that sunny Monday in July of last year. I had so dreaded the car-buying process that I'd put it off again and again. Finally, I decided to just start taking some test drives and work my way up to the actual sale. After I'd driven a couple of imports, I noticed the Saturn dealer a block away and, although that wasn't a brand on my list, I decided to stop there and take a practice drive. Four hours later, I was driving my new Saturn home. This came about with none of the pressure that often accompanies buying a car. The salesman went out of his way to locate the perfect car for me and made buying it easy.

The Saturn story is really a study in Success by Doing Things Better. Although this company is a division of the venerable automaker General Motors, they have carved out a niche by not being associated with the parent company. In fact, when the Saturn division came into being, they headquartered in Tennessee, not in Detroit with the rest of the line. From the moment they began selling cars in 1991, Saturn created customer loyalty.

Not only did they make a fine automobile, they added lots of personal touches. From their no-haggle selling policy to their customer reunions, Saturn did things their own way. Not all of these personal touches are grand. One of my personal favorites is the free car wash that comes with any visit to the dealer. Need an oil change? The car comes back sparkling. Need to wait for your car? The spotless customer lounge is comfortable, loaded with a wide variety of reading material and coffee. Got a question? Calls are returned promptly and questions answered thoroughly. Doesn't that sound like the way every business should be run?

## Actions Speak Louder

Many businesses use mottoes that declare that they care about their customers but the reality doesn't always line up. If you truly want to serve others and make doing business with you a pleasure, a little imagination backed up with action is far more effective.

I was having lunch at a busy restaurant in Denver, Colorado, last year when I noticed that people leaving the place all seemed to be eating ice cream. Glancing around, I saw a sign in the back announcing free ice cream cones. After I'd helped myself to one, I saw the manager standing behind the cash register and I went over and said, "This is a great idea."

He smiled and said, "Yes, people seem to love it. We don't spend one penny on advertising and we don't really have to. It probably costs us a lot less to give away ice cream but it creates so much good will that people keep coming back and tell their friends about us, too."

## It's Not Just the Perks

Ice cream cones and carwashes won't make a business successful if the essential product or service is a dud, of course. Those personal touches can go a long way, however, if the reason people come to your business in the first place is a Class A experience. Consumers can tell the difference between a gift that's offered generously and one that's intended as a bribe. The free carwash wouldn't be so delightful if Saturn hadn't made the entire process of doing business with them such a pleasure.

**It's Not About Size**
"No one is too big to be courteous," said Jerome Knight, "but some are too small." The smallest of businesses can follow the example of their bigger brothers and sisters who make the effort to delight their customers with small favors. I remember a woman who had a mail order book business who had beautiful bookmarks printed that were included in each order. Even the welcoming way in which you answer the telephone or respond quickly to e-mail shows a respect for the other person. So does sending thank-you notes to clients or those who give you a referral. These are all little things that can make a big difference.

Happy customers who say nice things about your business aren't the only benefit of adding value to your enterprise. Television legend Ed Sullivan saw another reward for behaving with kindness. "If you do a good job for others," he said, "you heal yourself at the same time, because a dose of joy is a spiritual cure. It transcends all barriers."

*To Affirm:* Small acts of kindness are a daily event in my business.

*To Consider:* What have you seen that made another's business positively memorable? Is there something you do in your business that elicits a response from your customers? Pass it on, if you'd like to share.

# A Business for Fun

*I think that the best investment that you can make is to start a business that is so much fun that you don't care if you go broke. With this approach, you can be certain of success.*
Phil Laut

"Everybody's workin' for the weekend," declares an old Lover Boy song. Look at the exodus on the highways leading out of any city on a Friday afternoon and it appears that for many people the weekend means a great escape, a contrast to the monotony of their work week. There's no more popular way to squander your life than to spend week after week waiting for it to be over. That's a strong indication that many people have never entertained the possibility that work can be a source of joy and even entertainment.

## If It's a Drag, Try Spending Money
A woman once called to tell me how thrilled she was with her new life as an artist. Then she confessed, "I find that I need far less money to live on and I finally realized that when I was working at a job I hated, I would spend the weekend shopping, hoping to buy something that would make me feel good enough to go back to work on Monday." Terry's story is not rare or unique but, as we all know, no amount of money or stuff can compensate for a boring life.

## The Paradigm Shift

In the old way of thinking, work was viewed as a means to an end: we trade our time for money which can be used to purchase a bit of pleasure. The new entrepreneurial thinking rejects this notion flat out. Instead of working to support things, to buy more stuff that might bring some temporary relief, we've turned things around and realized that we can set it up so our things support us. It's a far healthier attitude. We know we've really made it when we find ourselves getting paid to do things we previously had to pay to do.

Rod spent years in a corporate job while dreaming of being a full-time nature photographer. Today he is an award-winning photographer and he has expanded his business to include traveling around the United States teaching others about nature photography. His passion not only supports him in taking photographs that he sells, he also has the fun of sharing this passion with others who want to learn and improve. And he gets paid to travel besides.

Then there's the doctor I know who discovered his two great passions were learning about wine and spending time in Bali. Today he lives most of the year in this paradise and operates a successful wine import business there.

## Stop Saving, Start Creating

Coming to a place where your business totally supports your dreams may be a gradual process but it's worth including in your plans. Last summer I met a woman in Texas who shared my passion for Venice. Her primary business was life coaching but she'd started another profit center importing Venetian glass beads. "I suppose you're obliged to go to Italy on a regular basis to keep up your inventory," I joked. She assured me this was true.

Whether you are longing to spend time in Maui, dress regularly in a tuxedo, lounge at a spa or eat in fabulous restaurants on a weekly basis, I can promise you that somewhere, someone is doing these things and earning money at the same time. I want to challenge you to think about a really wild dream you may be keeping, one that you think you'd need to finance through other means such as saving enough money to do it. Start brainstorming ways in which you could actually be paid to live out this dream.

For instance, I have always loved the theater. When I first moved to Minneapolis, I discovered that the highly respected Guthrie Theater had a need for backstage tour guides. I applied and was soon standing on that famous stage every weekend sharing my love of the theater with visitors. Not only did I get paid for each tour, I also got four tickets to every production which made me very popular with my friends. There was another bonus in this for me; since I was spending most of my time as a freelance editor and writer this kept my public speaking skills from rusting. Best of all, it started me thinking about the connection between passion, creativity and money.

**A Powerful Tool**
Get in the habit of responding to the promptings of any dream by putting your entrepreneurial spirit on the case. There will still be times, of course, when you'll come up with a funding

idea that's separate from the dream itself. Still, there will be numerous times when you find yourself delighted and amazed to be in the midst of a dream that's supporting itself. You might find a good starting point is adopting this definition from actor Warren Beatty: "Success is when you don't know if you're working or playing."

*To Affirm:* My business supports me in getting paid to have fun.

*To Consider:* List all the ways in which you've been paid to do what you love most. How can you make the list longer? Consider, too, how a business that is essentially fun and satisfying elevates even the mundane tasks to a higher level.

# Showing Up

*Honeybees depend not only on physical contact with the colony, but also require its social companionship and support. Isolate a honeybee from her sisters and she will soon die.*

from *The Queen Must Die: And Other Affairs of Bees and Men*

Master P is the richest man in hip-hop music with a fortune estimated at over $330 million. His life in Beverly Hills with his wife and children is a far cry from his early days. Master P began life as Percy Miller growing up with two brothers in a violent area of New Orleans. One of those brothers chose life on the streets and was eventually murdered. The other brother is serving a long jail sentence. How did Master P create a life so radically different from his siblings? He attributes part of his success to having a deep desire for a life unlike the violent ones that surrounded him.

Once the motivation for change took hold, he settled on the entrepreneurial life as the ticket to his dreams. He took a $10,000 inheritance from his grandfather and cut his first album. Selling CDs from the trunk of his car, he built a strong fan base and the business grew from there. "There comes a point," he says, "when you realize that anything is possible. You just have to be willing to do it." Even his company name is a reminder of his belief: No Limits.

Master P isn't the first entrepreneur to discover how powerful the human mind can be when directed at a goal. Neither is he the first to recognize that in order to achieve his dreams he had to leave his dreambashing environment behind. Most of us face far less difficult challenges.

## The Power of Connection

Years ago, I watched a tiny little network marketing company grow into a national organization. This was not a get-rich-quick venture and many of those who ultimately succeeded invested a great deal of time before seeing much money. Because the company was founded by a man who understood much about mind power, he invented many ways to help people grow from the inside out.

One of those tools (although it wasn't ever called that) was organizing regular company events and meetings. Since the sales force was scattered across the country, most people had to incur travel expenses to attend. Repeatedly, I noticed, those who invested their time and money—even when the meetings weren't especially exciting—were the ones who enjoyed lasting success. By regularly gathering with others who shared their vision, they were sending a strong message to both their conscious and subconscious minds that this dream mattered. Spending time in the company of others who are forward-thinking can have a powerful, albeit invisible, impact on our ultimate success.

## Pay Attention

I am reminded almost daily that entrepreneurs think differently than people who are stuck in a job. In the area of money, for instance, Dreambuilders have a distinct take on things. Someone who has a fixed income mentality might dream of traveling and decide to scrimp and save for some faraway trip. Given the same dream, the entrepreneurs among us will start generating creative ideas that will fund such an adventure—and maybe even bring a profit. It's the enormous difference that only comes from living your life as cause, rather than effect. As an entrepreneurial friend of mine just said, "There's always a way to do the things you really want to do."

"If you want to be successful," goes an old slogan, "do what successful people do." Few people seem to pay much attention to the attributes and actions of those who achieve their dreams. Yet when we take the time to show up where other Dreambuilders are gathered, we have an opportunity to study first hand how they think and act.

Comedian Martin Short wrote a wonderful essay in *Time* magazine about the turning point in his life. He had moved to Los Angeles but was adrift. On the day that his own doubts and fears were the strongest, someone invited him to go to an improv show. To be polite, Short accepted, although he didn't want to go. He writes, "That show changed my life. The actors were improvising and my mind was going with them. For the first time, I realized that I could channel the way I could be funny at a party into my onstage role. But before that evening, I had never put the pieces together. I had never seen my potential."

**A Simple Action**
Want to see more of your dreams come true? It might be easier

than you think. If you can only take one action, here's the one: transplant yourself into a dreambuilding environment as often as possible. Gather with others who are motivated and proactive. Listen to inspiring speakers and read eloquent authors who have taken a higher path. Share ideas with forward-thinking people.

When you regularly show up for your dreams, they'll start showing up for you.

*To Affirm:* I welcome the insights I gain by spending time with positive Dreambuilders.

*To Consider:* Is there a time when you reluctantly showed up somewhere and came away with an unexpected gift? How can you create more opportunities for yourself to show up in helpful places?

# Fanning Your Creative Flame

*Creative activity could be described as a type of learning process where teacher and pupil are located within the same individual.*
Arthur Koestler

A student once described a creative flurry she was having by saying, "My mind is like a popcorn popper. The ideas just keep coming and coming." I always think of that when I'm having a similar burst of ideas. But why do these creative splurges occur in the first place?

Although I have read numerous books on creativity, I can't recall a single instance where reading about the creative process set off any fireworks. That's not to say that reading about creativity is wasted time. I'm fascinated by insights into the creative process but I find that my own imagination really gets moving by having contact with other people who are bringing their own unique vision to life. I notice that my own idea explosions happen after encounters with creative people. Try some of these ideas and see what impact they have on your own creativity.

## Practice Selective Awareness

I don't understand people who brag that they never watch television or read a newspaper because the news is too dreadful. Much of it is dreadful, of course, but there are good ideas that also manage to find their way to the media, too, and any creative self-bosser should be tuned in as part of their idea-gathering. Besides, isn't tuning out the world the work of cults and other mind control groups? Creative folks are connected, not isolated, from the global community.

Paying attention to the media can stimulate new ideas or affirm thoughts you've had. For instance, a friend once amused me by telling me she'd thrown a birthday party for her dogs. Apparently she's not the only one who wants to celebrate the birth of a beloved friend. A story on television spotlighted a company called Pooch Party Catering. If I hadn't seen that story, I would never have known that my friend had a potential business idea.

## Don't Hide Your Own Creative Interests

We've all had the experience of having our ideas trashed by someone who has never had an original thought to call their own. Consequently, it's sometimes easier to conceal our own creative drives and interests. However, as time goes on we become braver and suddenly understand the old saying about like attracting like as entrepreneurial folks begin showing up in our lives.

I was once scheduled to do a radio interview with a Seattle station prior to going there to do some seminars. I never know if a long-distance interviewer will be friendly or hostile so I was pleasantly surprised when the man who was about to interview me introduced himself to me during the commercial break. He wasn't just being hospitable; he was eager to tell me about a new business he'd started. "It's going gangbusters!" he exclaimed and I knew I was in friendly territory.

Trust that the more you let your light shine, the more supportive people you'll bring into your world, each adding their creative energy to your own.

**Let Other People's Creative Spirit Rub Off On You**
One weekend when I was out of town, two friends of mine attended a lecture given by travel guru Rick Steves. Although they'd gone there hoping to get some budget travel tips (which they did), they came away inspired by something else. As one of them put it, "Rick Steves really has a lot of profit centers!" Now students of Making a Living Without a Job may be the only ones to notice that aspect of Steves' work but they're also more likely than others to let that insight inspire their lives.

Advertising whiz Bernice Fitz-Gibbon created a stir with her exceptional ads for several New York City department stores a few decades back. In her biography, *Macy's, Gimbels and Me*, she has this to say about the creative process: "Where did you come from, ideas dear? Out of the everywhere into the here. Ideas pop out of books and the TV screen. They're tucked away in a childhood memory or in a play you saw sometime back. They spring from bird-watching or girl-watching. They burst forth from the mouths of little children or they sneak up on you in the middle of the night."

In other words, ideas are everywhere if only we pay attention. In a world full of creative people and ideas, there's no reason to deprive yourself of all the positive energy they put forth and the positive impact that will have on renewing your own creative spirit. The more you trust and value that creative spark, the brighter it will shine—which just might ignite someone else's creative flame.

*To Affirm:* I spend my time in ways that cause creative flurries.

*To Consider:* What, specifically, seems to trigger ideas for you? How frequently do you expose yourself to these creative catalysts?

# What You Say is What You Get

*The world is a better place as a result of Michelangelo not having said, "I don't do ceilings."*
Edward A. McCabe

A few Januarys ago, we Minnesotans enjoyed an unseasonably warm spell of weather. When normal subzero temperatures returned, our local weather forecaster announced the change by declaring, "Back to reality!" You've probably heard the same expression used by a returning vacationer going back to a ho-hum job.

While "Back to reality!" may be intended as an amusing comment—at least a harmless one—it strikes me as being anything but. When, I wonder, did Reality get such a bad reputation? Why would anyone label things that are mundane or unpleasant as Reality—implying that the good times must be Unreality.

## The Self-fulfilling Prophecy
For a long time now, psychologists have been telling us about the impact of the self-fulfilling prophecy. Our expectations, whether held as silent thoughts or spoken verbally, inevitably impact the results that we achieve. Knowing that we each have such power, why would anyone ignore or abuse it? Perhaps people either don't understand the connection—or don't know how powerful their thoughts and words are in shaping their

lives, even though we have evidence of that all around us and each of us has personal experiences that back that up.

A now-successful entrepreneur was telling me about the lowest point in his life. He had been evicted from his home and was thousands of dollars in debt. As he sat in his car pondering his financial future, he found himself thinking, "It takes money to make money." (This is an almost universally accepted platitude.) Since he had no money whatsoever, that thought was not encouraging.

As he continued to consider his options, a new thought came to him. "It takes ideas to make money," he surmised. Reframing the conventional wisdom led to a turning point and before long he was seeing plenty of evidence that ideas do, indeed, attract money.

Put yourself in this man's position. How would you behave if you truly believed that it takes money to make money? How would your behavior differ if you believed that ideas were more important? Anyone who's really paying attention would discover exactly what Paul Hawken describes so eloquently:"Money follows ideas. Money does not create anything at all, much less ideas and initiatives. Money goes where those qualities already are. Money follows, it does not lead."

**Whose Prophecy Do You Believe?**
There was a magazine ad that said, "Violence is the sound of ignorance." It's also ignorant to accept old platitudes about life without thinking them through. In fact, when you thoughtfully examine some familiar slogans, you'll come to the conclusion

that they're nothing more than someone else's self-fulfilling prophecy and need not apply to you at all if you chose to reject them.

Dr. Richard Wiseman spent eight years studying both lucky and unlucky people. His fascinating findings appear in his book *The Luck Factor*. The overriding evidence graphically demonstrates how luck is influenced by our own prophesying. Lucky people think quite differently than those who are repeatedly unfortunate. He writes, "Lucky people see any bad luck in their lives as being very short-lived. They simply shrug it off and don't let it affect their expectations about the future. Unlucky people are convinced that any good luck in their lives will only last for a short period of time and will quickly be followed by their regular dose of bad luck."

**Understanding Consequences**

As anyone who studies religion, philosophy or metaphysics knows, we live in a world that is governed by cause and effect. I've noticed that people who seem most ill at ease in life, who just don't get it, are those who have no comprehension that their words and actions always have a consequence. Instead of taking responsibility for their lives, they're a fountain of excuses. They're the people described by Richard Bach when he wrote, "Argue for your limitations and, sure enough, they're yours."

Our words, whether they're English, French or Swahili, become the blueprints for our lives. Just because they're intangible doesn't make them any less powerful. Listen to your own words. Even in casual conversation, what are you prophesying for yourself? While you're at it, monitor your thoughts, too, and when a self-limiting one passes through, stop yourself and replace it with one that truly expresses what you desire to have or to do.

It takes discipline and vigilance to master this but if you work at it you'll soon discover that there's no going Back to Reality since your reality is a terrific place you'd never want to leave for a moment.

*To Affirm:* Words create my reality.

*To Consider:* Keep your ears open and think about any self-fulfilling prophecies that you overhear. Explore further the difference between "It takes money to make money" and "It takes ideas to make money."

# Anthropology 101

*Of all the people whom I have studied, from city dwellers to cliff dwellers, I always find that at least 50 percent would prefer to have at least one jungle between themselves and their mothers-in-law.*
Margaret Mead

L ife is Good as an Entrepreneur" declared a recent headline in a Canadian newspaper. The accompanying story reported on a poll conducted by a leading financial institution. The survey interviewed 1,351 entrepreneurs and about half as many people who worked for someone else.

The results showed a startling amount of misconceptions on the part of non-entrepreneurs. For instance, more than half of small business owners said their stress levels were lower on their own; 71% of employees thought they would have more stress as an entrepreneur. The majority of employees thought they'd earn less money on their own, although that was not borne out in the responses from the small business owners. This poll vividly demonstrates that myths and falsehoods abound in the area of self-employment. The bank spokesperson said, "People underestimate the benefits of being an entrepreneur and overestimate the hard work and potential risk factors."

## Becoming an Entrepreneurial Anthropologist
If you're going to succeed in the entrepreneurial life, you need

to scout the truth for yourself and learn as much as you can about others who are sharing this path. In fact, you need to approach this like an anthropologist.

In case you've forgotten, anthropology is the study of mankind, especially of its origins, developments, customs and beliefs. These are all important aspects of the entrepreneurial life that are worthy of your time and attention. Be endlessly curious about how other self-bossers got started, how they grew their businesses, how they plan their time and what their belief system is. You could do the equivalent of a doctoral degree studying those success factors but, even as a part time hobby, entrepreneurial anthropology makes an inspiring pastime.

## Pay Attention

Without any special effort on my part, here are some of the things I uncovered in just the last week. The front page of my Sunday paper featured a story about the number of young people who are starting their own businesses. According to a survey conducted by the London Business School and Babson College in Massachusetts, one in every six young men and one in every 18 women aged 18 to 24 is involved in starting or running a new business. The article went on to talk about all the colleges that have added entrepreneurial programs just in that last several years. One professor said that when he started such a program in the 1980s, he got a great student response but parents would call, furious that he was putting such notions into their children's heads.

A few days later, Oprah Winfrey did a show about people

who had a good idea and saw it through. In addition to some wonderful success stories, she also had a competition with seven inventors who presented their ideas to the audience and talked about how they'd gotten their ideas. The word that popped up most throughout the show was "passion."

In the same week, *Time* magazine had a story about the growing bed and breakfast movement in the US with stories about several innkeepers. Another story in the same magazine talked about the growing popularity of bicycle tour companies. There was also an essay by singer Judy Collins about the turning point in her life when she picked up a guitar and knew her future was in folk music. "Immediately afterward, I felt ecstasy, as if a burden had been lifted. Creativity started flowing into all areas of my life."

Then I bumped into a neighbor I hadn't seen in weeks and he told me his uncle had started an exciting new business and he was helping get it launched. At the end of our conversation, I said, "I hope I run into you again in a couple of months and you have a big success story to tell me." He lit up and said he hoped so, too. I smiled all day thinking about his enthusiasm and the original idea that they were bringing to life.

### Field Study

Your anthropological studies will be enhanced with regular field trips. Many entrepreneurs pay too little attention to other businesses, especially those outside their own domain. What a shame. If you're an entrepreneur, these people are the members of your tribe. Get to know them better. Study their customs, ask them what got them started. Like a good anthropolgist, take field notes.

Where can this lead? "The true purpose of education," said writer Taylor Caldwell, "is to enlarge the soul, to widen the mind, to stimulate wonder, to give a new vision and understanding of the world, to excite the intellect, to awaken dormant faculties for the exaltation of the possessor." That's a big reward for following your curiosity.

*To Affirm:* I am endlessly curious about the entrepreneurial life.

*To Consider:* Have you come across any great stories in the media about someone who is self-employed? Do you have a notebook or file for saving the best ones? These can be great idea starters and sources of inspiration in the future.

# Easy Access

*How many a man has dated a new era in his life from the reading of a book? The book exists for us perchance which will explain our miracles and reveal new ones.*
Henry David Thoreau

Long before my daughter was born, I had a vision of parenting that mostly involved snuggling on the sofa and reading to my child. When Jennifer arrived, I began building a library of children's books, eagerly anticipating the day when we'd curl up together and read. What I didn't realize was that urging my daughter to love reading would provide a bonus I had not envisioned: now that she's an adult, we often have wonderful conversations about books we have both enjoyed.

Loving to read is not only the most blissful of occupations, it's also a critical factor in personal growth and equally essential to successful entrepreneurship. When I walk into a room or an office with bookshelves, I can't resist scanning the contents. We are partly what we read, after all, and a bookshelf can be as revealing as a personality test.

**The Seed of a Vision**
This was illustrated for me once again when I spent an evening with my friend Felicity in her new flat in London. Bookcases lined two walls of her dining area and as she prepared dinner I amused myself looking over the contents of her personal library. Not only

did I discover that Felicity and I share a fondness for many of the same books, our mutual passion for reading provided the main subject of conversation for the evening.

Eventually, we talked about books we'd read as children and she mentioned one she's loved as a young adult called *Champagne and Sandwiches*, the story of a divorced mother of two daughters who moved to a flat in Chelsea and made a creative project out of turning it into a home, despite having little money. When she told me this, I said, "And here you are living in a flat in Chelsea!"

"Yes," said Felicity, who grew up in New Zealand, "I think that book put the idea in my head that I wanted to live here and I never forgot it." Any avid book lover has stories like Felicity's about ideas they adopted from reading. Sadly, polls show that more and more of us are not reading. And it shows. People who don't read fail to understand the power of books to influence our lives for good. Or to transport us to places and ideas we'd never encounter any other way.

As any book lover discovers, the non-readers around them are often scornful of their passion for books. "Your family sees you as a lazy lump lying on the couch," wrote Cynthia Heimel, "propping a book up on your stomach, never realizing that you are really in the midst of an African safari that has just been charged by elephants or in the drawing room of a large English country house interrogating the butler about the body discovered on the Aubusson carpet."

## What Do You Need?
A few weeks ago, I did a talk on self-employment at a local

library. Early on in the talk, I told the audience, "The library is an entrepreneur's best friend." I wasn't just trying to flatter my hosts, however. Almost any time I've been stuck in my business, a library or bookstore held an idea or information or inspiration to get me moving again. It's the starting point for any new project and a never-fail source of on-going support. If I'm feeling a bit lethargic or my enthusiasm level is low, a trip to a place filled with books will turn things around at once.

Yet, hardly a week passes when I don't get a call or e-mail message from someone with a question that shows me that they haven't taken time to do the most fundamental bit of research for themselves.

I think entrepreneurs need to read widely and regularly. We need to find books of information that applies directly to our own business, of course, but we also need to read success stories, philosophy and personal development books as well. They're all there, you know, just waiting for the moment when you need them. Making time to include a daily reading session is one of the best investments you can make.

I hope you're one of those people who is part of the invisible network of those who are keeping reading alive. If so, you'll understand completely what John Russell meant when he wrote, "I cannot think of a greater blessing than to die in one's own bed, without warning or discomfort, on the last page of a new book that we most wanted to read."

*To Affirm:* The more I read, the bigger my world becomes.

## EASY ACCESS

*To Consider:* Got a favorite book that's made a difference in your entrepreneurial life?

What books would you recommend to someone just starting a business? To a fellow entrepreneur who's stuck?

# Dealing With an Up and Down Cash Flow

*All rising to a great place is by a winding stair.*
Francis Bacon

Carola Barn, a native of Greenwich, England, used to pass a junk store everyday when she walked her children to nursery school. She'd stop and buy something almost daily and eventually turned her acquisitive streak into a business of her own. She went on to open two shops which sold fabrics, dresses and anything else that caught her fancy. While she loved the changing aspect of her business, she said, "Everyone who owns a shop is manic depressive because you only feel as good as the shop is doing that day."

I'm not sure that I agree that our emotional well-being is dependent on the daily movement of our business but I do know that learning to manage cash flow fluctuations is a huge challenge for any entrepreneur. Learning to live with those ups and downs is important not only for our fiscal survival but also our emotional well-being, too. Let's consider a few things that can make that a bit easier.

## Get Smart About Money

Most of us have had little or no guidance in financial matters and, in fact, may have simply inherited our parent's beliefs, attitudes and limited knowledge. When you decide to educate yourself about money, you'll find there are plenty of willing authors to instruct you. The tricky part comes in finding a money expert who speaks to your sensibilities and situation. The majority of popular authors are writing for those with a fixed income mentality (that wouldn't be us) and their advice may not apply to those with irregular cash flows.

In the long run, you may find that reading metaphysical books such as those written by Catherine Ponder will give you a strong foundation in prosperity thinking. Then go on to an author like Suze Orman who combines practical money management with metaphysical thought.

**Watch Your Spending**
Don't spend yourself poor. Many new entrepreneurs get caught up in thinking it's all about creating a successful image so they pour too much money into things that count too little. That's the ego's approach. Spendthrift behavior, which is popular in many corporations, also may follow a new self-bosser who has left that milieu.

If feast follows famine, you may be tempted to pay off all of your old bills leaving yourself impoverished all over again. Designate a percentage of your income for debt reduction—recognizing that some months your debt will decrease by a larger amount than in slower times. Your mental health will be better if you hang on to some of your money and begin to see it accumulate.

**Take a New Approach to Debt**
Many of us grew up with parents who shunned the notion of

debt, paying cash for almost all purchases. In our credit drenched culture, others have accumulated massive debt with no notion of how they'll recover. As an entrepreneur, you'll find neither of these positions will support your dreams. A better way is to regard debt as an investment in your future, not a sign of irresponsibility. This is much easier to do when you are in love with your vision.

**Master Miscellaneous Income**
Keep a running list of emergency moneymakers. When things get tight, don't wait around for something to happen. Get busy and make it happen. Know, for instance, what you have to offer a temporary agency and let them help you through a cash crunch. The aforementioned Carola Barn installed an extra bathroom in her home in the event she decided to take in a lodger.

Creating odd income sources can be as good for the imagination as it is for the pocketbook. A friend of mine who lives on a busy street holds regular yard sales whenever he feels the need for extra cash. He stores boxes of things, all priced and ready to go, in his basement and keeps adding to his inventory. He could also sell some of his treasures on eBay, as another friend of mine does from time to time.

**Stay Creative**
Look for new ways of doing things using the resources you have. Catherine Ponder advises that if you're reduced to eating beans and wieners, get out your best china and dine by candlelight. The

more fun you can create with what you've got, the more you'll get. These exercises in using your imagination more and your pocketbook less can also lay down a foundation for ongoing profitability.

Equally important is to acknowledge the abundance you receive in unorthodox ways. Author Sondra Ray reminds us, "The basic law of the mind is the law of increase. If you concentrate on your surplus, your surplus will get bigger." So don't overlook the additional prosperity that comes your way when a friend takes you to lunch, the airline sends you a frequent flyer ticket or you win a night at the movies from your local radio station. All of these things add to your income just as money does.

*To Affirm:* My attitude does not depend on the state of my cash flow.

*To Consider:* Found a way of creating miscellaneous income— or heard about someone who has? Keep a list of emergency moneymakers to keep yourself from going into money panic when your cash flow is slower.

# Got Inspiration?

*The intellect is a bridge between islands of inspiration.*
Mike Myers

When I answered the phone the other evening, I was startled to hear my daughter wail, "I need inspiration!" I laughed and said, "You've come to the right place." I was also secretly delighted that she was wise enough to know that she could actively pursue inspiration when it seemed to be in short supply.

Only a few days earlier, I had a similar need. I woke up feeling a definite deficit of energy, enthusiasm and ideas. Since there were deadlines looming, I couldn't afford the luxury of wallowing in this uninspired state. I contemplated my options. Perhaps Vivaldi or Bach would lift my spirits, I thought, but neither seemed quite right. This was serious and I needed heavy duty help. There was only one possible solution. I needed *Layla*. Not the sweet, delicate shuffle version. This called for Derek and the Dominos. I grabbed my *Best of Eric Clapton* CD and headed for the post office. I managed to hear Layla three times in a row during my short drive and by the time I got back to my keyboard, I was ready to roll.

## In and Out

We all move in and out of our Inspiration Zones from moment to moment. Staying more in than out requires two basic things:

64

we need a high enough level of self-awareness to know which place we're occupying and we need to know the return route when we make a detour. We also need to know that being inspired is simply a matter of awakening to what's always there awaiting our recognition.

## Learning from a Master

Kaffe Fassett has taught me more about inspiration than anyone I can think of. Fassett grew up in the Big Sur area of northern California and left home to study painting briefly at the Boston School of Fine Arts. He dropped out and moved to London where his true calling emerged. Today he is a prolific designer of needlework, mosaics and other decorative arts but he says his mission is to rediscover creativity in himself and others—no matter what form it takes.

Known for his lavish use of color, Fassett said that when he first came to England he was astonished to learn there were so many shades of gray. In his book *Glorious Inspirations* he offers a fascinating look at a wide range of sources for his own work. What makes this book so intriguing is that it contains side-by-side photos of the original piece of art and then the Fassett design that it inspired.

Fassett personifies what artist Corita Kent meant when she wrote, "Creativity belongs to the artist in each of us. To create means to relate. The root meaning of the word art is 'to fit together' and we all do this every day. Not all of us are painters but we are all artists. Each time we fit things together we are creating, whether it is to make a loaf of bread, a child, a day."

**Close at Hand**

There's another paradox about the process of inspiration that also needs to be taken to heart. Although being inspired is a highly personal experience, it can be—and frequently is—triggered by reacting to something or someone outside ourselves. Whether it's music, a movie, a book or spending time in the company of a wise person, we need to know our own personal catalysts so we can call on them when the need arises. For Kaffe Fassett, it was the amazing Victoria and Albert Museum in London where he spent countless hours sketching, studying, refining his taste.

It's no good saying, "Ah, but I only feel inspired when I'm in Bali," if you rarely spend time there. You need to have accessible sources. Sometimes moving back into our Inspiration Zone requires that we give ourselves a change of scenery, of course, but if you look, you'll find plenty of stimulus all around you. From the moment I began reading Barbara Pym's books, I knew that she was a first class eavesdropper. The dialogue in her books sounds like real conversations—and, indeed, they were gleaned from listening to people talk on the bus, in restaurants and going about their lives. Pym just paid better attention.

On those days when you need inspiration, be bold in bringing it to bear on all those things that are yours to do. Be unwilling to stay outside your Zone too long knowing that your brightest and best contributions can only come from your relentlessly creative self staying tuned into the sights, sounds and feelings of life.

## GOT INSPIRATION?

*To Affirm:* I know what inspires me and I call upon it as needed.

*To Consider:* Make a list of ten surefire inspiration starters of your own. Include movies, music, places, people, books. Consult them when you've strayed from your Inspiration Zone and see how quickly they send you back where you belong.

# An Entrepreneurial Field Trip

*The world is like a book. He who stays home reads only one page.*
St. Augustine

One of my favorite television programs is *Actor's Studio*. Every week a different actor is interviewed in front of an audience made up of students from New York's Actor's Studio. The conversation often focuses on philosophy, craft and lessons learned. What's striking about the actors who are interviewed is that without fail they can quickly name other actors who inspired and influenced their work.

That capacity to name influential people, to know about the work of others in their field is not limited to successful actors, of course. People who are outstanding in every kind of endeavor share this trait: they have noticed, studied and been inspired by those who went before them. It's a trait that every entrepreneur needs to cultivate. Besides reading biographies and articles about fascinating businesspeople, seek out others who are living the entrepreneurial life and listen to what they have to say.

## A Trip With a Purpose

That's exactly what I did when I made a pilgrimage to Princeton, Wisconsin, a small town several hours' drive from my home. The impetus for this was stories I'd read about Tracy Porter and her wildly successful decorative arts business. After she opened a shop in tiny Princeton, several other creative entrepreneurs followed suit and I was eager to see how they have revitalized this community.

I arrived just before ten o'clock on a mid-week morning and found that Porter's shop was not yet open. I strolled up the street until I came to an enticing place called The Princeton Gardener. I entered the shop and was greeted by Julia Metcalf, the owner. After I had browsed and admired the visual feast which is the shop, I asked Metcalf how long she'd had her business. I was surprised when she said it was just three months old, since it had the settled look of an older enterprise. "Why did you start this business?" I asked.

She said she'd always loved gardening and has five gardens which were her passion. Then she told me that she had a dream about a house that was falling down but it was filled with little lights and in the center was a bigger light. It seemed to be about hidden potential, she said. "I woke up and knew that I was the light and I was supposed to be doing more to put that light out into the world. I knew that I was being told to use my creativity in a bigger way."

Without any certainty about how it would come together or how to finance it, Metcalf decided to open a shop to share her love of gardening. After she quit her job as a guidance counselor, things began to move quickly to make her vision a reality. Although this leap of faith hadn't always been easy, she said she was the happiest she'd ever been and was amazed at how quickly her business was growing. I left the shop feeling as if I'd taken a shower in pure, positive energy.

**Farther Down the Street**

My next stop was a funky home furnishings store called
Twister. Dennis Galtowitsch, the young man running the place,
welcomed me with a beaming smile. Twister was unlike any
store I'd seen before. "What's the focus of your store?" I asked.

"So I don't have to be an engineer anymore," he laughed.
Then he went on to explain that he and his wife had bought the
building which housed a hardware store. When he and his
tenant couldn't agree on the lease, he decided to take over the
space himself and open a store that sold things he and his wife
loved and used themselves. I was becoming more certain that
Princeton was a haven for enlightened entrepreneurs.

Eventually, I managed to spend time in the shop that had
started this revitalization fervor. Tracy and John Porter moved to
central Wisconsin after living in Chicago and working in the
corporate world. Tracy wanted to pursue her dream of turning her
art into a business and this shop is a tiny part of the Porter empire
that includes licensing her designs for everything from furniture
to greeting cards, as well as authoring lifestyle books. The day I
visited, the store was being run (with great enthusiasm) by Tracy
and John's sisters. They told me that Tracy's mother also gets into
the act, making this a real family affair.


**Take a Trip**

It doesn't take much to get me excited about the joys of free
enterprise, but I left this creative hotbed feeling inspired and
blessed by these strangers who shared their passions with me
and the world. There are small towns everywhere populated by

creative folks who are artistic entrepreneurs. Seek them out and make occasional visits to these places. Talk to the people who are living their own dreams and discover how much richer your life and your business will be for having met them.

*To Affirm:* I seek out and welcome inspiring creative thinkers.

*To Consider:* Tracy Porter says, "To live your passion is to treat yourself every day. Passion can be a constant positive force that moves you daily." How does a day lived from passion differ from one where passion is not present? Is passion practical or merely idealistic?

# Postponing Procrastination

*The crane that waited for the sea to sink and leave dried fish to feed him, died, I think.*
Hindu Proverb

When I told my Aunt Marge that I had fallen wildly in love with Italy, she sounded shocked. "Better than England?" she asked, as if I'd confessed to treason. "Oh, I still love England," I assured her. "But England is like a comfy old husband. Italy," I sighed, "is like a dangerous new lover."

My explanation was more than a metaphor. The week after I returned from Italy I was behaving like someone newly in love. I mooned around rewatching *Room With a View* so I could see the Tuscan poppy fields again. I imagined painting my walls terra cotta and adding frescoes, learning to speak fluent Italian and mastering Tuscan cuisine. I grew weepy over spaghetti sauce commercials. I avoided anything having to do with running my business. I was a goner.

After a week of this lovesick behavior, I began to get nervous. There were deadlines to meet, a newsletter to finish, new projects to begin. Since procrastination is not one of my normal vices, it took me by surprise. How was I going to get back on track? Did I even want to?

**The Art of Putting Things Off**
Perhaps there was something to learn from this, I decided. Don't

people tell me all the time that procrastination is their biggest challenge? I thought about people I know who habitually put things off. Since I was feeling quite uncomfortable by this time, I wondered how people who continually procrastinate could stand living with the discomfort that must always accompany them.

Then I realized that chronic procrastinators—the most skillful ones, anyway—are not idle. In fact, being terribly busy is often their main weapon. "Ah" they groan. "I have been run ragged lately." A closer look reveals that they are always running ragged—but not really getting anywhere. Spending time with a chronic procrastinator is not an energizing experience.

My cousin Ruth taught me more about procrastination than anyone I've known. Her life was littered with lists of things to be done but few things got crossed off the lists. I was perplexed by her inability to finish things (or even get started) until I realized that the cause of her procrastination was actually her perfectionism. Her fear of not doing things perfectly kept her from doing anything at all. When she died, leaving her estate in a huge mess, her family found notes throughout her house saying, "Rewrite my will."

## Moving Past The Sludge

Procrastination can afflict all of us for short periods of time. A dreaded chore, an unpleasant phone call or a serious case of daydreaming can render the most competent of us idle. For the most part, this is harmless enough. Unlike our chronically postponing peers, we'll eventually do what needs to be done. We just might be a tad late, that's all.

Whether procrastination is a big issue for you or only an infrequent visitor, it's helpful to understand this behavior so you won't find yourself on your deathbed with regrets over all the things you meant to do but didn't. (If this is a serious issue for you, I recommend Rita Emmet's *The Procrastinator's Handbook*. Incidentally, I wanted to quote from this book in this article but, when I checked with the library, all their copies were lost or overdue.)

Often, the tendency to put things off is simply a bad habit that's been cultivated over time. Yes, some procrastinators are lazy. Period. Others have such a lousy self-image that they lack the confidence to do even the simplest assignments. On a grander scale, fear and perfectionism (kindred spirits) render many folks inert. Then there are the ones who contend that they have too many ideas. This seems to be given as an explanation for accomplishing little, although I have a hard time following the logic. Whatever the cause, guilt eventually sets in and makes movement even harder.

Getting past procrastination begins with taking responsibility for it. No, others aren't making you do it; you are choosing not to find the time or resources to get at that undone project. When this happens to you, acknowledge that you're avoiding something that needs doing and then ask yourself if you know why you're shoving it aside. If fear, perfectionism or low self-esteem is the culprit, deal with that. Berating yourself won't work.

**Learn From Doers**

"Everything comes too late for those who only wait," said

Elbert Hubbard. What do non-procrastinators do that keeps them from putting things off? Most obviously, they are crystal clear about their priorities. They know what matters and what doesn't. They spend their time cautiously by measuring their time investment against what is most important to them. There's no disconnect between what they say is important and how they spend their time. When you know what lights up your life, knowing what to do becomes easy, effortless and natural— and done on time.

*To Affirm:* My priorities are clear and guide my use of time.

*To Consider:* How are your current priorities different from the ones you had ten years ago? Are your priorities really your own or influenced by someone else? When you find yourself procrastinating, how do you get past it?

# Seeking Hidden Opportunity

*He who bemoans the lack of opportunity, forgets
that small doors often open into large rooms.*
Rubin 'Hurricane' Carter

On May 24, 2002, I happened to see a Breaking News
story on CNN. An apartment building in Los Angeles
had suffered an explosion. The immediate cause was
unknown but, when they reported the address, I panicked.
This was the building where my daughter Jennie, her partner
Hector and their pug Emmit lived. I called Jennie's phones
but got no answer on either. The next forty-five minutes
were the longest of my life; then the call came saying they
were fine.

The next few weeks were chaotic because the building
was uninhabitable. Jennie and Hector had to quickly find
a new apartment, although most of their possessions were
impounded in the old place. It was months before things
settled down.

By May 24, 2003, Jennie and Hector were the new
owners of a gorgeous house that came with a magnificent
backyard garden. As the three of us were sitting on the
patio recently, we began talking about the dramatic events
of a year earlier. "That was the best day of my life," said
Hector, "although I didn't know it at the time." None of
us knew, of course, that the horrible events of that day

would mysteriously lead Jennie and Hector to this wonderful new home.

## Obstacle or Opportunity?

Almost everyone has a story about a loss or disappointment that turned out to be a blessing. The tricky part, for most of us, is to recognize that when our plans go awry, there may be greater forces at work. If we could remember that, there'd be far more rejoicing on a daily basis.

A woman in a seminar of mine told us that she'd been at a conference where she was doing two workshops on dealing with gambling addiction. When it came time for her first session, only one man showed up. Her second session attracted twenty-two participants. "If you hold a spiritual view," she said, "you know that things are working out perfectly. This lone man really needed my full attention. If he'd been in the bigger group, I never would have been able to help him as I did when he was the only one and felt free to talk openly about his problem."

Life only becomes an unending series of opportunities when we are willing to find the gift in every situation that comes our way.

## Two Dreambuilding Secrets

People who give up on their dreams are often unaware of two simple truths that govern success.

The first of these is that almost nobody can predict with certainty how much time it will take to accomplish a dream. Despite timelines and deadlines, our dreams often seem to possess a schedule of their own and it's our responsibility to hang in there for as long as it takes.

The other bit of astonishment is this: everything doesn't have to go right in order to achieve a dream. In fact, I'd be a bit suspicious if it all unfolds without a hitch. Dreams are here to teach us how to be more, not just have more. And those lessons don't come without errors and mishaps.

Stewart Emery tells a story about flying in the cockpit of a plane going to Hawaii and learning that every flight is a series of corrections. He says, "If we could see that we can get a 747 to Hawaii, having been in error 90 percent of the time, we might be a little less uptight about being in error ourselves. A sailboat cannot get from where it is to where it wants to go by traveling in a straight line. It has to zigzag. So, in terms of true course, it's always in error ... Somehow people have the notion that they are going to get away from failure, that they are going to succeed enough never to fail again. That option is simply not available; it is like trying to eat once and for all."

**Decide Right Now**
Before you encounter another delay or disappointment, decide to challenge yourself to find opportunities that are hidden, along with those which are obvious. While you're at it, give yourself permission to be in error much of the time. Know that ultimate success is a process of accumulation

and that you'll accumulate both victories and defeats along the way.

You'll understand what Jess Lair meant when he observed, "A fisherman is somebody who likes to fish. He has just about as good a day if he doesn't catch any fish as if he catches a hundred. He likes the process and the process is important. The goals and results and the fulfillment are simply inevitable outcomes and side issues of the process."

*To Affirm:* I will encounter enormous opportunity if I look for it.

*To Consider:* Recall a past situation that seemed like a disaster but led to something greater. How might you use that story to inspire someone else who is discouraged? What was the best day of your life so far? Did you know it at the time? List the hidden opportunities that you couldn't have anticipated in your own dreambuilding. Do something this week to celebrate how far you've already come.

# Starting Small, Thinking Big

*To climb steep hills requires slow pace at first.*
William Shakespeare

It had been two years since I'd seen my friend Belinda who lives in New York so I was looking forward to the afternoon we were going to spend together. Since I had no special requests, I left the planning up to her. As always, Belinda came up with the perfect activity. She suggested we visit the New York Historical Society Museum where there was an exhibit called Enterprising Women. She couldn't have found a better way to spend a rainy afternoon.

The first part of the exhibit had about a dozen video screens, each featuring a different woman entrepreneur. Some of them were famous, some were not. There was a short audio interview with each of them answering questions about their personal journey. On the floor in front of each screen was painted a pair of shoes so while listening to the audio you were figuratively standing in the subject's shoes.

The second part of the exhibit featured several early pioneering female entrepreneurs. Except for Katherine Graham, who took over *The Washington Post* when her husband died, every woman occupying space in the exhibit had started on a very small scale and risen to great heights through creativity and determination to succeed. After encountering these fascinating true stories, Belinda and I walked away feeling inspired and proud to be enterprising women ourselves.

## It Seems Obvious, But...

The women in this exhibit shared one of the most visible traits of the successful: a willingness to do things that others shun. That willingness includes getting started in the tiniest ways, if that's all that's possible, knowing that action creates results that accumulate over time. It's a trait that can be cultivated but is frequently neglected.

Valerie Young, a woman I met years ago in one of my seminars, got the idea to put together a retreat this summer in Colorado. She, Barbara Sher and I would be running the program. Almost the moment she began promoting this, Valerie began getting calls and e-mails from people objecting to the price. One woman wrote an especially hostile message, the essence of which was, "You've put together a program I want to attend but it's evil for you to expect me to pay that much for it." Understandably, Valerie was beginning to feel defensive.

One day I sent her a message which said, "Am I the only one who sees the irony in this? We're doing a seminar called *Making Dreams Happen* and people are telling us they aren't willing to find a way to make this one happen. This is just a goal-setting exercise, after all." I went on to propose that we hold a contest and see who could come up with the most innovative way of raising the money to attend. Valerie and Barbara Sher liked my idea so out it went to Valerie's online subscriber list. That made the crabby woman even angrier. How dare we suggest she work for this? Like many people, this woman would rather be pitiful than powerful.

**The Gift of Smallness**

The early days of a business bring a great opportunity to master things on a small scale. It's also a time to test our commitment. Are we really willing to do what needs to be done to bring our dream about? Filmmaker Spike Lee scraped together the money to make his first hit film, *She's Gotta Have It*, from many small sources. His grandmother invested in his dream but most of the funding came in bits and pieces. One of the things he did to raise money was gathering aluminum cans and selling them to a recycling center. That kind of creative problem-solving has served him well, although his financing channels have gotten more sophisticated.

**Thinking Big**

There was a television commercial that used to run where a woman says, "I'm the CEO of a major corporation. Well, actually it's a pet shop. But we're going to be big someday." Enjoying the early stages and holding on to a grander dream are essential. If you have a mental picture of great achievement and persist in making it real, the work you're doing now will take on a satisfaction and importance that are not possible if your only concerns are immediate gratification and instant results.

In his classic success book *As a Man Thinketh* (ignore the sexism here), James Allen wrote, "He who cherishes a beautiful vision, a lofty idea in his heart, will one day realize it. Cherish your visions. Cherish your ideals. Cherish the music that stirs in your heart, the beauty that forms in your mind, the loveliness that drapes your purest thoughts, for out of them will grow all delightful conditions, all heavenly environment. The dreamers are the saviors of the world."

*To Affirm:* I hold on to my ultimate vision.

*To Consider:* What is your idea of creating a big business? Do you want to build a conventional business with employees, branch offices and so forth? Or do you want to build a big little business that creates all sorts of abundance but remains a hands-on solo venture?

Either by reading or interviewing, find another example this week of someone who started small and went on to build the business of their dreams. What can you learn from their example?

# More Time, Please

*Now, here, you see, it takes all the running you can do to
keep in the same place. If you want to get to somewhere
else, you must run at least twice as fast as that!*
from *Through The Looking Glass* by Lewis Carroll

We Librans pride ourselves on being serenely balanced. No
wild extremes for us, is our motto.

Then why was I waking up with my Things To Do List flash-
ing through my mind before my eyes were even open? Why had
I written, "Get Oil changed" on my weekly list five weeks in a
row? Why was I repeatedly telling friends, "No, I can't come
out and play"? How had my life gotten so out of control?

Procrastination was not the cause of my downfall.
Underestimating the time it would take to complete several
projects had been my undoing. I needed expert advice in
reclaiming my time and I needed it now! Fortunately there are
a number of writers who have given time management a great
deal of thought and it seemed a good use of my time to consult
them.

## Prioritize
Alan Lakein's classic book, *How To Get Control of Your Time
and Your Life*, introduced me to the notion of determining
priorities. His system is simple and works wonderfully. Once
you've created a list of things you want to do, you rank them in

order of importance using only the letters A, B or C. This system is designed to keep you focused on the most important things in your life but it only works if you also understand consequences. In determining what item deserves an A, you also ask yourself, "What are the consequences if I don't do this?" Often you'll discover that in answering that question what first looked like an A item is actually a C.

Along those same lines is an idea I got from Charles Handy that has made an enormous difference in my life. That concept, which he writes about in *The Hungry Spirit*, is the idea of determining what "enough" means to you. He says, "My wife and I, since we became self-employed portfolio people, have regularly sat down each year and worked out what we need to live on. Since our standards of comfort and future financial security are quite high, so are our levels of enough. The simple act of doing this removes the temptation to maximize our income by working around the clock and the calendar, which is the dilemma of every self-employed person. This process has freed up a lot of our time because once the enough is guaranteed, there is no need or desire to spend time on making more than enough."

## Plan Ahead

Stephanie Winston's *Getting Organized* is another source of time tips. Gather your tools, equipment, research or whatever you need to complete a project before you start, Winston recommends. You lose both time and momentum if you have to keep stopping to search for something necessary to completion.

Learn to use little bits of unexpected time, too. Carry a memo pad and a book you want to read with you at all times to take advantage of those minutes when your doctor keeps you waiting or your lunch date is stuck in traffic. In fact, give up waiting time altogether by using these gifts of time to create or learn.

## Work Smarter

If your work area is a mess, start the new year by enlisting the aid of a professional organizer who can help you put things in order. Clutter and messy work areas cause confusion and irritability. Give yourself the advantage of working in an orderly environment. Know your own energy patterns and schedule creative work when your energy is highest, leaving routine chores for your less energetic moments. Become a consolidator. Return all phone calls during a specific time period rather than responding to each one. Combine errands. Keep file folders you use most often at your fingertips. While some people schedule every moment of their life, it makes more sense to use a diary or calendar to make dates with yourself alongside necessary appointments and deadlines.

## Super Smart

One of the very best things you can do is create at least one profit center that requires a minimum of your time and attention. While the popular term for this is passive income, it's a term that sounds slothful to me. The concept is brilliant, however. Whether it's collecting royalties on intellectual property you've created, rental income from property that you own or affiliate income from recommending someone else's products on your website, the idea is to have an income source that's nearly automatic. It's as close as we can get to buying time.

"People assume that they can find many ways to save time," says management expert Merrill Douglass. "This is an incorrect assumption for it is only when you focus on spending time that you can begin to use your time effectively." That's the smartest tip of all.

*To Affirm:* I invest my time wisely and receive a great return.

*To Consider:* Are there any tips, tools or insights you've discovered for using time wisely? Do you regularly assess how you spend your time and make changes where necessary?

# Small is Still Beautiful

*Build something, help something, save something. The possibilities are endless.*
Jack Lessinger

When I first realized that what I wanted to be was an entrepreneur, I headed to the library to begin my homework. As I delved into the few available books on how to start your own business, I became daunted and discouraged. Every book seemed to assume that all would-be business owners were aiming to create the next behemoth. I wasn't at all sure that's what I wanted to do.

Then Fate intervened and a marvelous, eye-opening book came into my life. That book was *Small is Beautiful: Economics as if People Mattered* by E. F. Schumacher. Dr. Schumacher, a British economist, wrote his book as a wake-up call during a time when the conventional wisdom insisted that growth was the only legitimate motive for a business. "Not so fast," warned the author.

He went on to cite Aldous Huxley who had written, "Suppose it becomes the acknowledged purpose of inventors and engineers to provide ordinary people with the means of doing profitable and intrinsically significant work, of helping men and women to achieve independence from bosses, so that they may become their own employers or members of a self-governing group working for subsistence and a local market. This would be a more humanly satisfying life for more people, a greater measure of genuine self-governing democracy and a blessed freedom." After reading those words, I breathed a loud sigh of relief and went on with the enthralling notion of creating my true and personal vision of a human-scaled business.

## Big Business Stays Small

While Schumacher's ideas largely went unnoticed in the United States, his philosophy influenced a few forward-thinking individuals. Paradoxically, the small is beautiful philosophy proved to be applicable even to large enterprises. To this day, billionaire Sir Richard Branson speaks fondly of following Schumacher's concepts in building his Virgin empire. Although Virgin is involved in numerous industries, Branson insists that his success is a result of the people with whom he surrounds himself and is committed to seeing that his employees have as much fun and share as much of the wealth as possible. "Fun is fundamental!" Branson declares often.

So is working on a small scale. One manifestation of this is Virgin's insistence on housing no more than 100 people in a single building. "Everybody should know each other so they can learn each other's strengths and weaknesses and feed off them," he explains. Branson is also constantly breaking up his companies and creating spinoffs to keep things as small as possible.

## Flaunting Smallness

Although initially I was sometimes embarrassed to admit that I was a one-person operation, I now proudly flaunt it. And, should anybody ask, I can also point out the advantages that are inherent with a small scale operation. Advantages such as speed. The difference between a big company and a little one, I've been saying for years, is the difference between a dinosaur and a jaguar. Small operations can make decisions quickly and act faster than most large companies. When the owner is the business, the level of service rises sharply, too. In studying customer service, for instance, I've discovered that the worst service providers are the ones where there's a great distance between those who own the business and those who deliver the service.

Even though we may have grown up with images of General Motors or IBM as the model of a successful enterprise, we're just beginning to get a lot smarter about what such organizations have contributed to damaging the human spirit. It was a problem Schumacher wrote extensively about, noting that human needs are infinite and infinitude can only be achieved on the spiritual realm. "Everywhere people ask, 'What can I actually do?'" Schumacher wrote. "The answer is as simple as it is disconcerting: we can, each of us, work to put our own inner house in order. The guidance we need for this work cannot be found in science or technology but it can still be found in the traditional wisdom of humankind."

## Long Live the Revolution

Happily, small scale enterprise is the new, healthy alternative that many are choosing instead of the old business model. We may not see workers revolting in the streets much these days but we are seeing a quiet revolution going on in cities and small towns all over the world. That revolution has led ordinary people to discover their own profitable and intrinsically significant work. Huxley and Schumacher would be proud of us. Even better, it's a revolution of the human spirit that's available to anyone ready to reclaim their soul and, in so doing, help create the new art form that is disguised as a small and beautiful business of their own.

*To Affirm:* I am creating a business that's the perfect size for me.

*To Consider:* Have you ever felt embarrassed about being a very small operation? Be clear about the advantages that a small business has over a large one and be bold about pointing those things out to those who think small equals insignificant.

# Beating the Work Alone Blues

*Those who would reap the blessings of freedom must be willing to undergo the fatigue of supporting it.*
Thomas Paine

There's a dark problem that faces everyone who starts a solo enterprise. To borrow from an old movie title, it's the loneliness of the long distance runner. There's no gathering around the water cooler, no buddies to gossip with at lunch, no co-workers telling you the latest joke. It's just you ... all by yourself. Sometimes it feels like everyone else is out playing ball while you're inside practising the piano.

The isolation factor looms larger if you're having a creative lull or business is quiet. It's enough to send you rushing to fill out a job application. Before you do anything so rash as that, consider ways in which you can counteract the aloneness by scheduling activities that guarantee you some quality interaction with other entrepreneurial folks. You have to be proactive about this or it won't happen. Here are a few ways to balance alone time with social time.

## Let's Meet
My friend Peter and I communicate by phone and e-mail several times a week. Once a month or so, we schedule time together at "our" Starbuck's where we might spend a couple of hours talking about our respective businesses. Could we handle the business on

the phone? Of course—but we both enjoy getting together and find that we leave with fresh energy and ideas.

Another great idea is to find a small group of other solo entrepreneurs and have a monthly brainstorming lunch or breakfast. Such relationships can be vital to your success.

## Take a Class

Seminars are a great place to meet like-minded people. Once a month—or more—take a short class or workshop that enhances your personal or business growth. If you show genuine interest in the other participants, you might make a new friend or connection. (This sounds so obvious but I've been watching and too many people don't make the effort to talk to strangers.) After all, you do want other lifelong learners in your circle, don't you? At the very least, you'll learn something new.

## Volunteer

Volunteering can be a great way to let others get to know you—while serving the common good. A man who sold insurance decided he was going to tithe his time by doing volunteer work four hours a week. As time went on, he kept on expanding his volunteer time until he was spending half of every week volunteering. Did his business suffer as a result? Not at all. In fact, his business grew primarily because of all the people he met as he went about helping out in volunteer activities.

## Take a Walk

Harvard Professor John Stilgoe teaches some of his most

important lessons by walking around with his students, getting them to notice what's in their own environment. He says, "Students come here with excellent verbal and math skills but they aren't very spontaneous. They need to know there's another way of knowing."

You can take a walk to revitalize yourself and get a bit of inspiration at the same time. Walk through a small business as if you're an anthropologist. Any ideas you can borrow? Anything that triggers a new thought in you? Notice little things. It's healthy to spend time in a successful environment—so walk around one as often as you can.

## Collaborate

When my daughter was in college, she and four friends planned a trip to Europe. By the time the trip rolled around, the others had dropped out leaving Jennie and her backpack to go it alone.

Despite her apprehension, she discovered that solo travel had many advantages. One of her best discoveries was making new friends along the way. They'd travel with her for a few days before parting company. She might be alone for a few days, then form another alliance. She decided this was more interesting than having a steady travel companion.

You can use the same idea in your business. Many entrepreneurs are eager to form partnerships when starting a business. Like any other close relationship, when it works, it's fabulous. When it doesn't it can distract from growing the business. Forming collaborations is a common sense alternative that eliminates many problems.

Unlike a partnership, a collaboration exists for a pre-determined time with the intention of accomplishing a specific goal. When the project is over, you can plan another project or go your separate ways without having the entanglement of a formal partnership.

"People are lonely because they build walls instead of bridges," said Joseph Newton. Paradoxical as it may seem, the way to have a great independent life is to leave room for inter-dependence.

*To Affirm:* I am finding creative and satisfying ways to expand my circle of connections.

*To Consider:* Have you regularly used any of these ideas to energize your own business? If so, what made the biggest impact?

Also, what do you think would happen to your current business if you regularly used these five suggestions?

# A Portable Reminder

*The mightiest works have been accomplished by those who have kept their ability to dream great dreams.*
Walter Bowie

Several years ago, my friend Chris came to visit me and began reading my copy of Stewart Emery's book *Actualizations*. She loved the book as much as I do but getting a copy was a bit of a challenge since the book had gone out of print and the Internet hadn't arrived to make locating one easy. Both of us scouted every used bookstore we visited looking for a copy.

After a five-year search, I finally located a copy which I sent off with the inscription, "Consider this a symbol that everything that's eluded us for the past five years is now ready to appear." If either of us ever became frustrated by some elusive goal, just remembering that we'd located the book caused us to relax.

### Find a Talisman
Any meaningful object, like Chris's book, makes an ideal talisman which can serve as a constant reminder of things we are working on in our lives and businesses. By its definition, a talisman is an object purported to bring good luck. Using a talisman to aid in goal achievement is not a new idea, of course.

When I was in Greece, I discovered shops which sold small metal plates engraved with a variety of pictures. I was told that these are used to enhance prayers. If someone was praying for a healing, for instance, they would buy one of these plates with a picture of the body part that needed aid. Other plates contained pictures of houses, boats and other objects of desire. I promptly purchased one to serve as a talisman for a long-range goal of mine.

### The Pragmatic Side

Author Ralph Charell points out that carrying a talisman can be a powerful aid in obtaining what you want. He writes, "Putting aside for the moment any consideration of the supernatural attributes or powers of talismans, and planting our feet firmly in the natural world of sensory data, there are a number of ways in which they may be useful. A talisman provides a convenient, portable, three-dimensional, concrete focus for galvanizing goal-directed thought into productive action. You should select the most appropriate object, one that would continually remind you of your specific goal."

Whether or not a talisman brings good luck is for you to decide. It's real purpose, it seems to me, is to add power to the mental processes involved in goal achievement. My friend Dan was an aspiring actor. One day I ran into him and he was wearing a stunning crystal necklace. As we began talking, he told me about an exciting role that he'd recently gotten. "Do you think your necklace is responsible?" I asked. "No," he smiled. "I think it's my talent. The crystal helps me remember to use it."

### Put it to Work

Think of one of your goals and imagine an appropriate symbol of that. Then find a small object that represents your goal and tuck it in your pocket or purse. Be sure, however, that you put it in a place where you will come across it frequently. When you do, take a moment to affirm that you have achieved your goal. After a short while, when you see the object it will automatically trigger that positive thought. Since we know that whatever we focus on will expand—and ultimately manifest in our lives— a talisman can speed up that process by focusing our mental attention more constantly than might happen otherwise.

Nobody succeeds beyond his or her wildest expectations unless he or she begins with some wild expectations. With a talisman at your fingertips, you'll have a constant reminder to keep your expectations high.

*To Affirm:* I am selecting the perfect talisman to keep me in touch with my dreams.

*To Consider:* A study found that the average American can identify 2,000 products by sight but can name fewer than ten species of trees. Could it be that a logo is a talisman of sorts?

What visual reminders can a small businessowner use that makes them memorable and recognizable?

# Love Thy Customers

*Love is the selfless promotion of the growth of the other.*
Milton Mayeroff

We Mac users are a loyal breed, fiercely sticking to our renegade computers in a pc world. We identify with the company slogan, "Think Different" and pride ourselves on not following the crowd. If I had ever been tempted to stray from Mac World, last week's experience won my heart forever.

When my computer crashed for the umpteenth time, I called the Apple Store and asked if they had a Genius Bar, a service I'd just learned about. They assured me that there were geniuses waiting to help me. Since the store is in a large mall, I was concerned about getting my computer lugged in from the parking lot. They'd anticipated that, too, and told me to give them a call on my cellphone when I arrived and they'd carry it in for me.

For the next hour and a half I sat on a stool watching resident genius Dave fiddle with my Mac. During that time, numerous people stopped to ask him questions which he patiently answered. I noticed everyone left smiling. "You get to make people happy all day, don't you?" I asked. "Yup, pretty much," he said. When he had finished working his magic, someone carried my computer back to the car for me and I drove home happy. Oh, yes, and the charge for all this service was zero.

When I told someone the story, she wondered how they could afford to do this for free. I pointed out that I'd just spent almost two hours in the store surrounded by gorgeous new computers. "When I get ready to buy my new one, where do you think I'll go?"

We might feel funny about calling it love but that's exactly the way that businesses build devoted long-term customers.

## Engage Your Customers

My favorite Christmas present a few years back was a mousepad with my daughter's baby picture on it. She had it made at a small print shop in her neighborhood. After the holidays, we made a trip to that shop so she could show me her picture on the wall. Along with photos of other customers who had purchased customized t-shirts, bumper stickers, etc. there was a Polaroid picture of Jennie holding up the mousepad. Although this shop is neither the most convenient nor least expensive, she now makes it a habit to return there whenever she needs printing or to send faxes. It's no coincidence that she's become a loyal customer. They're the only print shop that ever made her feel special.

Years ago, Napoleon Hill wrote in his classic *Think and Grow Rich*, "Men and women who market their services to the best advantage must recognize that they are employed by the public they serve. If they fail to service well, they pay by their loss of privilege of serving." It's still true.

## It's a Partnership

"The market is as much a part of your company as you are," author Paul Hawken believes. "After all, it represents one-half of the ledger. To succeed, your business must earn the permission of the marketplace. The customer must give your business permission to sell to him. I firmly believe that no concept is more important to an entrepreneur."

Hawken's position is, sadly, rare. But companies who value their customers and consider them partners in success become the exception that customers rave about. They also become the companies that grow, prosper and stay in business year after year.

### It's Love Actually

It's really the Golden Rule in action: treat customers exactly as you want to be treated. As Amazon.com founder Jeff Bezos has observed, "It's not our customers' job to stay awake nights figuring out how we can serve them better. That's our job. And we should do it so well that they never have to think about it."

When you get right down to it, the customer is a major success factor in any business. They deserve to be treated with respect and sincere appreciation. Doing so is not just good public relations, however. Really loving and caring about the people with whom you do business makes being an entrepreneur the satisfying and pleasurable activity it deserves to be. Wasn't that why you wanted to be in business in the first place?

*To Affirm:* I am devoted to creating successful partnerships with all my customers.

*To Consider:* When you are the customer, pay close attention to what works. When have you received service when you felt really valued? When have you had a customer who told you that your service was extraordinary? How had you created that?

# The Well-Furnished Mind

*Success isn't a result of spontaneous combustion. You must set yourself on fire.*
Arnold Glasgow

It's been over a half century since Dr. Norman Vincent Peale's *The Power of Positive Thinking* was first published. This book, which has never gone out of print, has sold almost as many copies as the Bible. Considering its widespread readership, we should be the most positive generation in the history of the world, harnessing this power to impact every aspect of our lives.

Even though many of us acknowledge a tangible benefit in positive thinking, there seems to be little evidence that positive thinking has invaded the lives of the majority. It takes great courage—and action—to shut out complainers and skeptics who are quick to say, "Positive thinking doesn't work." Those devotees of negative thinking are living proof that negative thinking also works.

Living a positive life has little to do with externals. It's totally an inside job—one that begins in our minds. "Since we are destined to live out our lives in the prison of our minds," said actor Peter Ustinov, "our one duty is to furnish it well." The good news is that we can renovate our minds or just touch things up a bit whenever we like.

## Be Conscious
Artist Corita Kent once painted a picture on which she wrote,

"There's a positive side and a negative side. At each moment you decide." Give some thought to the qualities of a positive attitude. What sort of results does being positive produce? How can you decide in favor of living on the positive side? If you do so, how will it change your inner and outer lives? How will it add to your ability to bring your dreams into being?

These are questions that cannot and should not be answered lightly. You also can't assume a positive posture if you are a victim of outside events and circumstances, reacting positively only when things go your way. Genuine positive thinking is not for fair-weather fans.

**Exercise Your Mind**
You know how sluggish your body gets when it isn't exercised. The same is true for your mind. Teach yourself to do something new. Enroll in a class and let someone else teach you something new. Studies have shown that people with a healthy curiosity not only live longer but are happier than their less curious counterparts because they are actively engaged in making new discoveries.

But the rewards of learning go even farther. A professor of anatomy at the University of California, Berkeley, Dr. Marion Diamond, spent two decades studying the effects of learning environments on rats. When they were taken out of typical laboratory cages and place in enriched environments—lots of rat toys and rat puzzles—the very structure of the rats' brains changed in as little as four days. These enriched rats solved mazes and puzzles faster than they could before landing in the toy-rich cages. They could handle more complex problems. By every measure, they got smarter.

There's an equally interesting downside: when enriched rats were placed again in ordinary cages, their brains changed again—they got dumber. Age didn't matter but the type of activity mattered a lot. Diamond's rats had to be actively involved. Just watching other rats playing did nothing at all for the brains of the spectator vermin.

So brain fitness comes from the process of learning, rather than what is actually learned. Although I haven't seen any specific studies on the subject, I suspect that computers have provided more exercise for more out of shape minds than almost any other invention in recent times. In our rapidly changing technological world, there is no shortage of new things to learn.

**Practice Makes Better**

If you haven't yet reached a mental state that is totally positive (few ever do), give yourself a daily challenge to improve. Set aside 30-60 minutes at approximately the same time every day when you make a conscious effort to act positively—no matter what happens during that time. To begin with, pick a time that is usually not stressful or challenging. You can work up to practising positive thinking while you're driving in traffic later as you become more proficient.

At first, you may find this difficult to maintain but, with consistent practice, you'll soon have new skills that will creep into your life at other times of the day as well. This isn't just a flimsy pleasantry, however. This is a basic success skill.

In fact, consider what business guru Tom Peters has to say: "My hypothesis is the world is loaded with smart people, the world is loaded with energetic people and there is even a large subset called smart, energetic people. But unless you are smart, energetic and turned on, you haven't got a snowball's chance in hell."

*To Affirm:* My mind is furnished with the highest and best thoughts.

*To Consider:* Have you experienced the power of positive thinking in your own life? Do you have a technique or tool that helps you cultivate a positive attitude? Or do you believe positive thinking is for the naive?

# On Getting Advice

*Nothing is easier than fault-finding; no talent, no self-denial, no brains, no character are required to set up in the grumbling business.*
Robert West

Steve Merritt grew up in Iowa dreaming of a life of social activism. When he told his high school counselor that he wanted to find a solution to world hunger, the counselor scoffed and said he needed a more practical career plan. Following that advice, he ended up in the cable television industry earning lots of money and little personal satisfaction.

Eventually Merritt turned his growing discontent into a life-changing event and today he happily heads up a community garden project in California. He sees his new role as a manifestation of the adage, "Think globally, act locally."

Merritt's story is a great reminder of the dangers of well-meaning advice. Now I have nothing against advice *per se*. Obviously, I'm in the advice business. But there are some things to consider when receiving advice so you can sort the wheat from the chaff.

### Rule #1: Consider the Source

The most important thing about receiving advice is that you know your source and trust them. I was once reading a newsletter written by a woman I have watched build a lovely business. One of the articles really struck me as special and I e-mailed her suggesting that she send it to some other publications. (Okay, I confess that violates my own policy of giving unsolicited advice.) She wrote back saying that she had thought about submitting some of her newsletter material to other markets but someone had told her that she couldn't do that since it was already published.

I was flabbergasted. Who would have erroneously advised her? If it was a professional writer giving the advice, they would have known about resubmitting material. If it wasn't a professional writer who told her this, why would she have taken the advice?

This isn't an isolated incident. We've all probably allowed false advice to influence us. Sometimes it happens because the advice-giver sounds authoritative and so we look no further. At other times, maybe out of laziness, we accept negative or discouraging words as an excuse for not giving something a try. And sometimes we just don't know if the advice is accurate. (This is a particularly new and thorny problem caused by the Internet where advice is posted but not edited or verified.)

## Rule #2 : Get a Second Opinion

While too many opinions or too much advice can serve to confuse us, if you're exploring unknown territory some serious research is in order before setting out. Get advice from people who know what they're talking about—and then get a back-up opinion or two. I once got e-mail from a woman who said that all of her life she'd wanted to be a professional caricaturist but everyone told her she couldn't make her living doing that. I asked her if she was getting advice from other caricaturists. Having numerous opinions from uninformed sources doesn't make the information accurate. Having several opinions from experienced sources is another matter altogether.

## Rule #3: Make the Most of It

When you ask the advice of another person, your initial role is to be a quiet listener or to ask clarifying questions. Whether or not you act upon the advice is a matter for a later time. When you're trying to make a decision or need information so you can proceed with a decision you've already made, seeking outside input is just part of the information-gathering process. Sifting comes after you've got all the information collected.

When you are the recipient of advice, whether you use it or not, don't forget to say thank you. I mention that only because I'm stunned by the number of people who don't bother with this courtesy. Keep in mind this advice from Abraham Lincoln: "When you ask from a stranger that which is of interest only to yourself, always enclose a stamp."

The world is full of teachers, experts and amateur advisors—with varying qualifications. Jess Lair once said, "When I'm working on my life, I want the very best teachers I can find." Finding the right ones to help you learn what you need to know so you can move forward in your own life is not to be taken lightly. The experience of others can save us time, add deeper insights, prevent us from making costly mistakes. Ask only those who can help, not hinder, your success.

# ON GETTING ADVICE

*To Affirm:* I eagerly listen to advice from reliable sources.

*To Consider:* What's the best advice you've ever gotten? The worst? When you need advice, how do you go about finding it? How do you react to unsolicited advice?

# Ride More Waves

*My first teacher told me, "You only have to practice on the days that you eat."*
Hilary Hahn

My brother Jim lives in California and is an avid surfer. He's also 57 years old. My sisters and I like to point out to him that although we've seen his wet suit and surfboard, none of us have ever seen him in the water. He points out that surfing isn't really a spectator sport.

When we were chatting recently, he said, "I was driving to the beach yesterday morning and it was still dark. I was thinking, 'Why am I doing this?'" "You're doing it so you can have a lively old age," I suggested. He laughed and said, "You know I surf better now than I did thirty years ago." I pointed out that he'd also been disciplined about keeping at it. "I still love it," he said, then added, "The more waves you ride, the more goes in the bank. It all adds up."

## Riding to Mastery
So what do you want to be better at doing thirty (or ten) years from now? Whatever your answer is, the time to start working on it is right now. In his wonderful little book, *Mastery*, George Leonard says, "We tend to assume that mastery requires a special ticket available only to those born with exceptional abilities. But mastery isn't reserved for the super-

talented or even those who are fortunate enough to have gotten an early start. It's available to anyone who is willing to get on the path and stay on it—regardless of age, sex or previous experience."

Perhaps you've never given mastery much thought. We live in a time of instant results and instant gratification—not a culture that's conducive to taking on a project and sticking with it for years. This quick results attitude aborts many wonderful ideas. I recall a friend abandoning a project by saying, "There doesn't seem to be much energy around it." I thought he was quitting before he ever got started but his explanation also implied that it was only worth doing if he was getting a huge response from other people.

**First Do it Badly**

If you want to master something, you must be willing to enter at beginner's level. Our egos often resist this notion. In my *Establish Yourself as an Expert* class, I suggest that people get some media practice by doing interviews with local media. This idea is often met with disdain. My students want to head straight for Oprah. I patiently point out that they'll do a much better job if they've had lots of practice before Oprah calls.

If you're working on something that truly requires mastery, you'll keep returning to beginner's level at every step of the process. Olympic skater John Curry once talked about hitting a plateau in his skating. No matter how long and hard he practiced, he wasn't moving to the next level. One day on the ice, he realized that as he was skating, his internal message to himself was, "I'm not falling down. I'm not falling down." When he challenged that and attempted moves that caused him to fall, his performance began to soar ahead.

## Keep Making Deposits

To my astonishment, I suddenly got an itch to learn to play poker. I started by getting some books from the library, asking everyone I knew if they could teach me, and watching poker tournaments on television. On one of the programs, I heard the announcer say, "This game takes a minute to learn and a lifetime to master." That was very appealing to me.

How much richer would our lives all be if we approached every aspect as being fair game for mastery? Instead of just going through the motions, what if we decided to master cooking, parenting, friendship, our business? This is not the same as being a perfectionist. It's consciously looking for the learning in even the smallest activity. It's being awake for the entire show. It's being willing to inch ahead knowing, like Jim, that it all adds up.

As George Leonard reminds us, "What you are made up of is mostly unused potential. It is your evolutionary destiny to learn and keep on learning as long as you live."

If you didn't memorize these words the last time I quoted them, do it now because Mick Jagger summed it up perfectly when he said, "You've got to sing every day so you can build up to being, like you know, absolutely brilliant."

*To Affirm:* The path of mastery is a path worth taking.

# Ride More Waves

*To Consider:* What have you abandoned too soon? What is fascinating enough to you that you'd be willing to undertake now and keep going? Can you imagine what doing so would look like ten years from now?

# Magic Moments

*You are a performer. Your work is theatre. Now act accordingly.*
The Experience Economy

Everyone who works at Disney World is a member of the cast. Whether wearing a costume or sweeping the streets, Disney workers are reminded daily of the role they play in making their audience's visit a memorable one. Disney may be more theatrical but the best businesses—the ones where everyone seems to be enjoying themselves—are those that understand that we're all in show business.

This idea that work is theater is explored in Pine and Gilmore's provocative book, *The Experience Economy*. At first glance it may seem like a radical, or at the very least duplicitous, notion to suggest that business and theater share the same purpose but, as the authors point out, any work a customer observes directly is an act of theater. That one idea, if fully understood, could turn the most ordinary business into an unforgettable one.

## Geeks on Stage

Whenever I see a distinctive black and white VW Beetle hurtling down the highway, I think, "There goes The Geek Squad making the world safer for technology." Founded by Robert Stephens in 1994, this computer repair firm has set itself apart from the dozens of other businesses doing similar work.

In less than ten years this company, which started with one geek and a mountain bike, has grown far beyond the borders of Minnesota with new squads popping up in cities around the country.

The eye-catching company vehicles are just one of the props they use. All Geeks wear a uniform consisting of short-sleeved white shirts, clip-on ties and plastic pocket protectors. They also carry an official badge declaring themselves a member of the Squad.

Visit their Web site (www.geeksquad.com) and you'll see how much fun they're having with their declared mission of achieving world domination. At the bottom of the screen is a rotating list of citizen rights that include such things as, "You have the right to read more novels and fewer manuals," and "You have the right to spark a movement with one e-mail." There's also a section on the site called Random Acts of Technology. Here's a company that understands that high tech can also be high touch.

All this silliness isn't merely a bunch of geeky guys having fun, however. There's a brilliant concept behind the showmanship. As every computer owner knows, nothing has the capacity to frustrate like an unruly computer and on the day you need a repair person, it's not a happy day. The Geek Squad knows that and uses humor to make their visits less traumatic.

## Solo Performers

Those of us who are one-person businesses have an even greater challenge since we play many roles in running our businesses.

Nevertheless, a one-person show can be as entertaining or enlightening as one with a huge cast.

You don't need to wear a costume (although we all actually do) or drive a custom-painted car in order to create a theatrical experience for your customers. Consider for a moment one of the basic opportunities every business has to connect or disconnect with their audience: the telephone. Like most people, I talk to a lot of voice messaging systems and I'm appalled at how unwelcoming many of them are. Who wants to do business with someone who sounds apathetic on their first encounter? Unfortunately, many people answer their phones with that same lack of enthusiasm. Any playwright or author knows how important it is to hook the audience in the first few seconds. The same is true in our contact with potential customers and clients.

### It's All About the Audience

I've never thought that visiting an automobile dealership was a particularly delightful experience until a year and a half ago when I became a Saturn owner. Even going in for a simple oil change is an entertaining event. The moment I drive into the service area, several people surround my car and begin vacuuming the carpet. No matter how small the service or repair, the car is returned to me fresh from the carwash. The waiting area is comfortable and clearly designed to make me feel like an invited guest.

Great companies like Saturn understand that in order to build a business that stands out there needs to be more for the customer than just a product or service: there's always the opportunity to create a memorable experience. The question then is whether you'll bore, enchant or insult your audience. The winners in the Experience Economy are always striving to give their best performance.

*To Affirm:* My business is a wonderful vehicle for delivering memorable experiences.

*To Consider:* Imagine advertising your business the way that movies advertise in newspapers. What adjectives (followed by exclamation points) would appear in your ad today? What adjectives would you love to see that aren't there yet?

# Cultivating Interdependence

*The discovery of a way of being that worked for me came
as a result of spending time with men and women who act
in the world with excellence, joy and service.*
Stewart Emery

Entrepreneurs have a well-deserved reputation for being independent. This can be both a strength and a weakness. When I was having dinner with a friend of mine recently (not an entrepreneur herself), I found myself stiffening when she said, "You are going to have to hire help."

Thinking about my reaction later, I realized that I am not adverse to having help; it's the hiring part I resist. Long ago I decided I did not want to have a business that had employees. It's a decision that has remained.

Be that as it may, it does not mean that I have to do everything myself. I started counting up all the people who directly and indirectly contribute to my business and the list was longer than I'd realized. Who are the people who help me live the life of my dreams?

## My Support Staff

There's Georgia who sees to it that I get back and forth from the airport and does all sorts of other helpful things for me and my business. Georgia also kept things running smoothly for the *Running an Inspired Business* seminar in Las Vegas. Then there is the ever-so-patient tech team of Peter, Niki and Blair who make it possible for me to function in cyberspace. Of course, the US Postal Service, United Parcel Service, the guy who makes my CDs and audiotapes along with two print shops also play critical roles in my business, as do the owners and staffs of a dozen or more independent adult education centers where I teach.

Those are the obvious people who help me out. I have no idea how many unknown people make a contribution by telling others about my work. I was reminded of this during a consultation recently when the woman said she'd given away numerous copies of my book—including one to her former employer—and was urging anyone she met who mentioned self-employment to get a copy for themselves. I could also count media people who have interviewed me, booksellers that stock and sell my book, website owners who link to my site and organizations that invite me to speak as part of my support staff. In fact, if I really pay attention, it's easy to believe that the entire world is helping me grow my business.

**The Path of Growth**

Psychologists tell us that the maturing process happens in three stages. We go from being dependent to being independent to being interdependent. Creating mutually supportive relationships is a higher level of growth than being totally self-reliant.

Our working lives follow the same path. Most of us start out working for someone else, go out on our own and may be quite alone at first, then mature into a business that interacts with other businesses and individuals. If you come to see those relationships as links in your chain of good, you'll see the wisdom of keeping those links in good repair.

**Into Practice**

There are some simple things you can do to use your business as a vehicle for supporting the entrepreneurial spirit of the world. For starters, look for ways to do business with other small businesses. You might pay a little more to shop at an independent bookseller or hardware store but do it anyway. When author Barbara Sher learned that her neighborhood florist was in danger of going out of business, she went home and e-mailed her large database inviting them to order flowers from the shop and send them to her. She explained how wonderful the flower shop was and what a bright spot it was in her New York neighborhood. She assured us that even a small order would help. I was on the phone within minutes of reading her request. That's the kind of practical support that we can offer one another.

Small businessowners need to create as many reciprocal arrangements as they can. My tax accountant, print shop and audio producer all get regular referrals from me. That's an easy and natural way to show appreciation.

There's nothing wrong with showing appreciation in other ways as well. Who doesn't like getting a note expressing gratitude? Genuine appreciation builds strong personal relationships and it does the same for business relationships. "In ordinary life," said Dietrich Bonhoeffer, "we hardly realize that we receive a great deal more than we give, and that it is only with gratitude that life becomes rich."

*To Affirm:* Cultivating healthy relationships is a wise use of time.

*To Consider:* In what ways do you cultivate interdependence in your business? Do you have a particularly satisfying relationship that supports you? Anyone you'd like to publicly praise?

# Bold and Brave

*Fortune is not on the side of the faint-hearted.*
Sophocles

When a reporter asked basketball great Bill Russell how he and his teammates overcame their fear on the courts, the legendary player retorted, "We don't overcome fear. We are experts in terror management."

It's easy to attribute outstanding success to fearlessness but things don't get accomplished because fear is absent: they get accomplished because fear is acknowledged and managed. As management consultant Jonathan Odell writes, "Besides lions and tigers and creepy things in the night, most of the things that frighten us are in our heads. We literally scare ourselves silly with thoughts of humiliation, failure and rejection, all based on memories of past experiences. It is no coincidence that the first signs of fear and memory occur in the same stage of infant development. We are not afraid until we have the capacity to remember how things used to be."

Odell goes on to say, "We can spend hours trying to defeat our fear by training our self-talk, reprogramming our beliefs and developing courage in the comfort of our living rooms. Courage, however is not a product of the harbor; it is born in the storms at sea. Courage is a decision made in the face of fear, not in the absence of it."

**Avoid Avoidance**

Many—perhaps the majority—of people attempt to manage fear by avoiding situations or circumstances that will produce fear and the inevitable discomfort that goes with it. Speaking in public, taking a stand, trying something new are totally out of the realm of their consideration. While avoidance may save us a few uncomfortable moments, it also prevents us from living as big and rich a life as we could. Avoiding fear is living life in beige.

The truth is, no one is fearless. The difference between people is their decision to act in the face of fear. Or, as Stewart Emery told an interviewer, "The difference between successful people and unsuccessful people is that successful people have fear and are successful. Unsuccessful people just have fear." The question then is do you use fear as a reason to retreat or as information about how to proceed?

**Challenge as a Priority**

One of the most effective means of terror management is to issue challenges to yourself on a daily basis. That's the path taken by Doug Tompkins who has accomplished much by constantly trying to outperform himself. Both in entrepreneurial and conservation circles Doug Tompkins is something of a legendary figure. A high-school dropout and gifted alpinist whose devotion to climbing kept him mostly in the mountains, he founded, at the age of twenty-two, an outdoor gear and clothing company called The North Face. He later sold that business, and with then-wife Susie Tompkins built a small clothing operation into a global retail powerhouse, Esprit.

During his years building Esprit, Tompkins developed a reputation for defying convention. He refused to meet with bankers, avoided lawyers and wouldn't sign documents. He was fond of something he called MBA—management by being absent. He surrounded his employees with signs bearing his personal mottos: LIFE IS ENTERTAINMENT; SURVIVAL IS A GAME and NO DETAIL IS SMALL. He told his employees not to be surprised, "If I ask you what books you've read to stimulate your brains, what adventures you've had to stimulate your sense of life, what love affair was fulfilling."

Tompkins sold his half of Esprit in 1990 (for an estimated $125 million) and plunged full-time into conservation work, endowing the Foundation for Deep Ecology and purchasing wild lands in Chile. He and his spouse Kris McDivitt Tompkins have worked tirelessly to acquire more wild habitat and build a world-class nature reserve entirely through private means. With their 750,000-acre Pumalin Parque nearing completion, they will eventually transfer ownership of their lands to the people of Chile to become that country's most spectacular National Park.

Apparently, courage isn't just needed when our lives are in jeopardy. It's also the companion of the visionary.

**A Powerful Virtue**
Developing courage also involves knowing the difference between things that should be feared and those that shouldn't. But that's not the only consideration here. As Doug Tompkins showed us, our own business can be an on-going program for

building courage. We are tested constantly to do things we've never done before or to handle situations where we're going to be rejected. Our willingness to do those things has a big impact on the results we produce but that isn't the biggest reward for being bold. As Winston Churchill, who knew a thing or two about acting in the face of fear, pointed out, "Courage is rightly esteemed as the first of human qualities because it is the quality which guarantees all others." Do you need another reason for building courage in every possible way?

*To Affirm:* It's through acting in the face of fear that I develop boldness.

*To Consider:* Notice something that frightens you and act in the face of that fear. How does it add to your confidence to do so? Also helpful is to learn to distinguish between genuine fear and self-doubt (which is often mistaken for fear).

# Ask Better Questions

*Ask and it shall be given you; seek and you shall find; knock and it shall be opened unto you.*
Matthew 7:7

We humans are born question askers. Listen to any toddler and you'll hear a stream of questions about any subject that catches their attention. "Why?" is the most frequently used word in their vocabularies. During the days when I taught high school English, I used to say that my idea of hell was being in a roomful of teenagers all screaming, "Do we have to?" It was a question that often erupted after I gave a challenging assignment.

Questions are such a common part of everyday communication that most people don't give much thought to them. But I'd like you to pay more attention. I started to do so when I noticed that a popular television talk show host seemed to turn the most fascinating guests into complete bores. As I watched more closely, I discovered that his questions often led to deadends, giving his guests no place to go or no story to tell.

People who have charisma, who draw others to themselves, usually have a reputation for being good listeners. Part of their secret, it seems to me, is that they ask great questions to begin with and then give their full attention to the answer, prodding and encouraging when necessary. They make people feel valued because they listen to the answers.

## More Than a Social Skill

Asking good questions isn't just a way to win friends and influence people, however. It's an overlooked key to success. Tama Kieves was a Harvard Law School graduate who was living her parents' dream as a successful attorney. She was good at it, too, with a rosy future and expanding income. Despite her outward success, she was unhappy practising law and longed to write, teach and explore. She wrestled privately with leaving the career and prestige that she had worked for.

One day she was having lunch with a trusted friend and confided in him the dilemma she was facing. "That's silly, Ms. Harvard lawyer," he said. "If you're this successful doing work you don't love, what could you do with work you do love?" The right question comes with great power and Tama was smart enough to pay attention when her friend made the query. Those wise words blasted Tama out of her Comfort Zone and into a new life filled with joy, satisfaction and plenty of insecurity.

## Question Your Way to Your Dreams

Not all questions are so illuminating. Many, in fact, stop us dead in our tracks. "How are you going to do that?" or "Why haven't I gotten farther?" are the kinds of questions that lead us down the path of doubt, not dreams. Learning to ask better questions of ourselves can get us headed in the right direction and keep us moving forward.

Mark Victor Hansen and Robert Allen, the authors of *The One Minute Millionaire*, point out that when we ask the wrong questions we condemn ourselves to living below our potential. They write, "If you ask yourself, 'How do I earn or create a million dollars?' your mind goes to work to discover the answer. Your mind is compelled to work ceaselessly until a satisfactory answer is found. Note that most individuals ask themselves questions like these: 'How do I get a job, salary or work?' or 'Can I earn $50,000 doing this?' The wrong question will generate the wrong result or a less than outstanding outcome. Questions predetermine the answer. The size of your question determines the size of your answer. Few people ever ask million-dollar earning, inventing, innovating, generating and creating questions."

## Why Not Try This?

If you keep a journal or idea notebook, start making a list of provocative questions you'd like answered in your own life. Ask them in the most compelling way you can think of. "How can I deliver the most fabulous service possible?" is a lot more intriguing than, "How can I give better service?" Consider questions about spirituality, relationships, personal growth and improving the overall quality of life, as well as questions about creating the most brilliant business possible.

Keep adding to the list and leave room after each question for the answers to come. Be willing, also, to be patient in receiving your answers. As writer Zora Neale Hurston reminds us, "There are years that ask questions and years that answer." The important thing is to ask the best questions to begin with—the ones that are worthy of your dreams.

## ASK BETTER QUESTIONS

*To Affirm:* The size of my question determines the size of my answer.

*To Discuss:* What are some big questions for a Dreambuilder to ask? How do you decide when to ask others for help in finding an answer?

# Always Enough

*You need to make a life rather than a living. You might be much happier making one-third of your income, but coming from a place of beingness that brings joy to your soul.*
Neale Donald Walsch

Coco Chanel, who said a lot of smart things, once observed, "There are people who have money and people who are rich." It's not hard to figure out which is which. The people whom I think of as rich are those who have a practical prosperity consciousness. My sister Margaret is such a person. I have long admired her ability to use whatever resources she has to the max.

When we were in a pottery shop in Sienna, Italy, Margaret was captivated by a beautiful plate. We left the shop to contemplate making such a hefty purchase and as she considered the pros and cons she said, "I have noticed that when I'm anxious about money and start skimping, I never have any money. When I'm relaxed about it, I always have enough."

I believe that's true for everyone, whether we know it as well as Margaret does or not. This Wealth-as-a-State-of-Mind attitude is not an easy thing to master in a world that often speaks loudly about scarcity and impoverishment. In fact, most people are unaware that their thinking influences their sense of wealth or lack—far more than their bank balance does.

## A Lesson in Lack

Years ago, when I was living in Santa Barbara, I went out one day to begin my Christmas shopping. Although I seldom carried much cash, that day I had more of it with me than usual. From the moment I got downtown, I began to experience anxiety. Everyone looked like a potential mugger. The distress was so intense that I went home without buying anything.

Shortly thereafter, I realized that I had a deep belief about money that went, "If I have money, people will harm me." I decided I needed to change my belief and, also, discover what other thoughts I had buried away that kept me from enjoying financial ease.

I began reading Catherine Ponder's classic, *The Dynamic Laws of Prosperity* every day. I also was greatly helped by the writings of Sondra Ray. One of her suggestions was to start carrying a large bill, eventually working up to $100. The purpose, she explained, was that every time you spent money and saw the large bill in your wallet you'd be sending a powerful message to your subconscious which was, "I have plenty. I have a surplus of money." Within months, I went from the seeing the world as full of muggers to carrying large amounts of money with ease. It felt like a huge victory over an old adversary.

Since money is a source of so much upheaval, each of us needs to thoughtfully examine our own attitudes and beliefs and create the healthiest approach we can muster. Going along with unchallenged ideas about money, old scripts from our parents, will not do the trick.

**Another Way to be Rich**

Consider, then, this story from business guru Charles Handy: "'How much money do you earn?' I used to ask friends in my competitive days. It seemed the best way of comparing progress in life. I was brought up short by one who replied, 'Enough.' 'What do you mean—enough?' I asked. 'What I say—enough. I work out what I need and that's what I make sure I earn. Why bother to make more? How much sugar do you buy in a year?' he turned and asked me. 'I have no idea,' I said. He replied, 'But I bet that there's always sugar in your house when you need it. Money is like sugar, no point in hoarding it. It usually goes bad or you have to make quite unnecessary cakes to use it up.'

"Crazy man, I thought; but as I grew older I realized the sense in what he had said. He knew what he wanted out of life. He wasn't using money as a substitute for uncertainty."

There's a fascinating study in Jean Chatzky's book *You Don't Have to Be Rich* which looks at the connection between money and happiness. What her study found is that money and happiness are linked—but only up to the point at which we have enough. After that point, more money does not translate into more happiness. This is not an indictment against having money, of course. It's simply a challenge to you to give thoughtful reflection to your own definition of "enough."

*To Affirm:* I naturally create a life of enough money, joy and satisfaction.

## Always Enough

*To Consider:* Has your notion of what is enough been influenced by outside forces such as advertising, keeping up with the Joneses, etc.? How could getting a clear picture of your ideal life help you establish what enough means and, also, help you figure out how to create that?

# Practising Benign Neglect

*A field that has rested gives a bountiful crop.*
Ovid

Sometimes our businesses can be so demanding that we seem to be working around the clock. We buy into the old notion that working incessantly is the road to success and feel guilty if we're not up to our necks in chores. There's plenty of evidence to suggest that this is not the way to accomplish great things.

What if we could make our businesses better by neglecting them from time to time? What if we shifted our attention to something else throughout the day? What if we developed the confidence to let go and let our businesses grow by themselves a bit? Action, followed by reflection, followed by more action is the method practiced by many of the most creative and productive.

It's a process we can adapt to running our own enterprises.

## The Da Vinci Mode

In *How To Think Like Leonardo da Vinci*, author Michael Gelb points out that great geniuses frequently accomplish more when they work less. When Leonardo was painting *The Last Supper*, for instance, he annoyed his patron by painting feverishly for hours, then he would sit for hours in quiet contemplation. The artist had to continually defend this way of working to an impatient taskmaster. Gelb suggests we need to do the same.

"Almost everyone has experienced sleeping on a problem and awakening with a solution. But incubation is most effective when you alternate, as Leonardo did, between periods of intense, focused work and rest. Without periods of intense work, focused work, there is nothing to be incubated ... Neuroscientists estimate that your unconscious database outweighs the conscious on an order exceeding ten million to one. This database is the source of your creative potential. In other words, a part of you is much smarter than you are. The wisest people regularly consult that smartest part." There are numerous ways you can begin putting this system to work.

## Give Your Brain a Break

Throughout the day, give yourself ten minute brain breaks. Listen to music, do some stretching, doodle, stare out the window. Walk away from what you're doing and come back to it. As Leonardo said, "It is well that you should often leave off work because when you come back to it you are a better judge."

A brain break doesn't need to be long in order to be effective but there are ways you can expand it. If you're feeling really bold, take a nap as often as you dare. Many businesses are discovering that their workers perform better after a daily nap. Thomas Edison knew that, too, and was an enthusiastic practitioner. Studies have shown that a short nap, no longer than twenty minutes, is more refreshing than a longer snooze.

## Observe a Sabbath

Although many religions encourage their followers to spend a day each week in spiritual contemplation, author Wayne Muller points out that you needn't be an adherent of such a faith to do so. In fact, he says, we need not even schedule an entire day each week. Sabbath time can be a Sabbath afternoon, a Sabbath hour, a Sabbath walk. The point is to use this time of sacred rest to refresh our bodies and minds, restore our creativity and regain our birthright of inner happiness.

This is also where it's an advantage to have diverse interests. Setting side one day, or part of a day, each week to shift gears can be both fun and therapeutic. Get up from your computer and have a vigorous game of tennis or stop building stone walls and write in a journal. The point is to spend a significant amount of time doing something that's the polar opposite of what you do the majority of the time.

## Go on a Retreat

Every year, Microsoft founder Bill Gates takes himself away for a week-long reading retreat. You don't have to be a billionaire to do the same. A reading respite is a great idea that you can adopt if you want to have a longer time for contemplation.

A pair of writer friends of mine find that when they are working on a joint project, a rustic retreat eliminates distractions and encourages new ideas. As every traveler knows, a change of scenery can uncover fresh thoughts. We all grow stale—or worse—if we remain stuck to the same place day after day. "People who cannot find time for recreation," warned John Wanamaker, "are obliged sooner or later to find time for illness."

There are many ways to practice benign neglect but it takes

discipline to put this into your schedule. If you master it, you will save yourself years of hard work—and build a body of work that is satisfying and bountiful.

*To Affirm:* My life is calm and balanced as I practice action followed by reflection followed by action.

*To Consider:* Do you have a favorite way of taking a brain break? Do you have a ritual Sabbath?

Consider fresh ways you can consciously refresh and restore yourself on a daily basis.

# How to Stand Out in a Crowd

*Since each of us is one-of-a-kind, the market, for all its
supposed predictability, is actually vulnerable to falling in
love with any of us at any time.*
Julia Cameron

It's been a long time since I was in high school but one thing
hasn't changed much: adolescents still want to be like everyone
else. Teenagers dress alike, listen to the same music, love the
same movies. Being different is a surefire way to become
unpopular, the most dreaded horror of teen life. While conformity
is comforting in adolescence, it only serves a purpose in human
development if it's treated as a stopover in the journey.
Unfortunately, many adults suffer from arrested development
and spend years trying to conform. Who's going to notice a
conformist?

Probably the media won't pay attention and neither will
many other people.

## Who Gets Noticed and Why

On weekends when I have an out of town seminar, I usually
pick up a copy of *People* magazine at the airport. Even though
the cover of the magazine usually features a celebrity, I find that
the stories I enjoy the most are about people who aren't famous,
just fascinating.

One issue included a section called Starting Over and

featured six people who had made dramatic life changes. Four of the six of them became self-employed. One of the others, a former chef in upscale restaurants in New York and Washington DC, reached the point where (in his own words) he'd, "Been there, sautéed that." Wanting to do something more meaningful, he now cooks upscale cuisine in a soup kitchen. The other person, Omar El Nasser, abandoned his cubicle in a windowless office in Buffalo and now works as a cowboy in Montana. When an ex-colleague saw a picture of Nasser on horseback, he hung it above his own desk and labeled the image, "Omar's Cubicle."

For all of these people, Starting Over was about putting themselves on The Road Less Traveled. It's a message that seems to be popping up all over the place these days.

## Another Great Story

One of the most inspiring stories I've seen lately on television was about Danny Meyer. In his late teens, Meyer spent a year and a half in Italy filling journals with notes on restaurants he visited there. Besides taking note of the food, he sketched light fixtures he liked, flooring that caught his fancy, and studied the ambiance of various establishments.

Today he owns five popular restaurants in New York, places that regularly top the Zagat restaurant survey. In addition, he's revived a neighborhood near his businesses by spearheading such things as a year-long outdoor produce market that serves the residents and restaurants around Union Square. As the television piece pointed out, he's created his own village within New York.

His passion and philosophy of making a difference right where he is makes him a standout.

## It's Obvious, Isn't It?

If you want to stand out from the crowd you first have to leave the crowd. It's a message philosophers have espoused for centuries, but only the most determined among us has paid attention. While we can be inspired by the Danny Meyers of this world, we fail if we try to duplicate their path. It's only when we can revel in our uniqueness that we start making the real contribution that is ours to make. Not only will that lead us to optimal joy, it might even bring the media to our door.

*To Affirm:* I celebrate everything that is unique about me.

*To Consider:* Make a list of five adjectives that describe you. Do negative or positive words first spring to mind? Make a list of five outrageously positive words that describe you. How can those qualities become the trademarks of your business? Imagine your story in *People* magazine (or some similar story-filled publication). What would you like the headline to say?

# The Key to Lasting Success

*If you renovate your life, you can inherit the world.*
Wally Lamb

Few people had heard of Wally Lamb or read his novel *She's Come Undone* but that all changed with a phone call he received one day while he was loading the washing machine. The caller was Oprah Winfrey telling him that she had selected his story for her Book Club. Like others so selected, Lamb's book went on to bestselling success. His subsequent book was also a big seller.

Although this may look like another case of Overnight Success, the truth is that Lamb, a high school English teacher, had been quietly and diligently perfecting his craft for years. Perhaps that's why Lamb took his newfound fame in stride. Others who have found their fortunes rising rapidly have not always managed so gracefully.

## Waiting Won't Do It

Our culture has long been fascinated with the notion of Overnight Fame and Fortune. It's a dangerous dream. Several years ago, my friend Chris and I met a talented clothing designer. We thought he deserved a lot more success than he was having and offered our assistance. Our efforts came to a halt when he confided that he was waiting for some wealthy person to discover him and become his patron. We never managed to convince our reluctant protégé to take a proactive approach to building his business and, I suspect, he's still waiting.

We know that waiting for a fairy godmother to show up is not one of the seven habits of highly effective people. Like all those who think life will begin if only they win the lottery, time and talent is being squandered while waiting for something big to happen which will catapult them forward.

## What Will Do It

At the same time, everyone of us has it within our power to conceive of a dream that we can begin enjoying at once. Right where you are, with exactly the resources you now have, you can begin to invest your precious moments on goals that are richly satisfying all along the way. Those who have discovered this secret are on their way to building such a strong foundation that when great financial rewards come along, they handle it with grace and ease. Like Wally Lamb, they've grown into their success and it's a perfect fit.

"Genius is simply a long patience," contended French naturalist Georges Buffon. It seems to me that nearly everything worth having in life is the result of a long patience, a patience that many run out of before they ever come within spitting distance of their dreams. On the other hand, those who accomplish great things understand that it will be a long term process.

## Think Like an Architect

For several years, whenever I visited my family in California, I observed the construction of the monumental Getty Center which soars above the freeway on a Los Angeles hilltop. With each visit, I could see small progress. When it finally opened, media people from around the world turned up to marvel.

This amazing modern wonder was designed by Richard Meier who devoted nearly a decade of his life to the Getty project, leaving his comfortable life in New York to live in a ramshackle house on the edge of the building site. The architect is not just fascinated by gigantic buildings, however. Meier is also a voracious collector of personal memorabilia and on his frequent flights between coasts would amuse himself by filling notebooks with collages of ticket stubs, memos and mementos he'd collected. Apparently, Meier has found a creative way to balance the pressures of being responsible for one of the most discussed buildings of our time with maintaining respect for personal memories. In a way, he's keeping his own foundation in good order.

It's easy to dismiss small deeds as insignificant but, as any architect knows, the most complex building requires a long patience. You don't have to design buildings to see the truth of this. The moment you dream a dream and begin to build it, you become the architect of your future. And a great future begins with a strong foundation. Without it, there can be no lasting success.

*To Affirm:* I am willing to invest long patience in building my dreams.

*To Consider:* What kinds of things do you think are important for building a foundation for your dreams? What are the rewards of getting the foundation in place? What are the penalties for not doing so?

# One of a Kind

*The principle mark of genius is not perfection but originality, the opening of new frontiers.*
Arthur Koestler

Given her penchant for funky long skirts and chunky jewelry, if you saw Margie Bergstrom walking down the street you might think, "There goes an artist." While there's plenty about her that's creative, her business is accounting and tax preparation, not art. For the past fifteen years, Margie's been my tax preparer. I found her through the recommendation of a friend and have sent dozens of other clients to her. I don't think anyone I've told about her has ever gone elsewhere once they've worked with her.

She was just getting started when I began using her services and she ran her business out of her home which made her particularly attractive to me. In those early years, I'd make my annual trek to her house and be greeted by her assistant who would seat me in the pleasant living room, bring me cookies and coffee and draw my attention to the magazines placed on the coffee table. By the time the previous client was finished, I was so relaxed that I almost forgot the onerous reason I was there.

**Warming Up a Cold Business**
As much as I liked her and looked forward to hearing about her latest sailing expedition, I didn't have much experience with tax

preparers so I didn't realize how unique she really was. Then around our fourth year together, she called to ask if I would do a talk on marketing to her tax professionals organization. I agreed and discovered a fairly humorless group (note: if you're an accountant and you're reading this, I'm sure that wouldn't apply to you). At the end of my talk, in which I'd mentioned Margie's high touch approach to business, she came up to me and said, "I am almost afraid to tell you this but my business has grown too big for my house so I'm moving into an office." It was at this point that Margie's husband quit his long-time corporate job and joined the family firm.

The first time that I went to her new office, I was expecting it to be cold and clinical. I should have known better. I walked into a waiting area where hot cider and coffee sat alongside a plate of cookies. The magazine rack was filled with travel and lifestyle publications. There wasn't a financial magazine in sight. This year, she's added a small fountain and gorgeous orchid plant to the waiting room. Framed pictures of her travels are scattered around the office.

## Creating Rapport

Since we only see each other once a year, my appointment is also filled with chatting about our comings and goings in the previous time. Margie and her husband, avid sailors, are working their way through all of the Great Lakes. She gets wistful talking about Santorini, her favorite destination. At the end of tax season, they treat their staff to an exotic vacation—one that may include sailing. This year I was teasing her about her ancient adding machine. She said, "I've already found the pop artist who's going to paint it for me. Then when it finally dies, I'll just hang it on the wall as a piece of art."

Margie is also skillful at breaking the news about her client's tax situation. When I frowned to learn that I owed more than expected, she smiled and said, "This is the only place where a good year is bad." Since I have long promised myself I would never resent having to pay a large tax bill, I saw that my intention was being challenged and attempted to be cheerful. In fact, I stopped at the florist's on the way home and bought myself a gorgeous orchid to celebrate my good year.

## Lessons in Uniqueness

So what can we learn from Margie? Plenty, I'd say. Part of her success is the result of her being very good at what she does but there are lots of accountants who have good skills. It's the personal touch that has skyrocketed her business from a handful of clients to over two thousand of us. As Margie brilliantly demonstrates, a strong sense of self leads to building a one-of-a-kind business by providing the details only you can supply.

"No one can possibly achieve any real and lasting success in business, "warned J. Paul Getty, "by being a conformist." It's obvious that Margie Bergstrom would heartily agree.

*To Affirm:* Creating a one-of-a-kind business is the key to my success.

*To Consider:* Think of three other businesses that are similar to yours. What makes each of them unique? How can you add an extra dimension of uniqueness to your business? Give some thought this week to how you create rapport with clients and prospective customers. How are your listening skills? How sensitive are you to the problems and upsets they bring with them?

What do you think someone who saw you walking down the street would think you do for a living? Is that the message you're wanting them to get?

# Feeding Your Creative Spirit

*A person's mind stretched to a new idea can never return to its original dimensions.*
Oliver Wendell Holmes

My friend Georgia is going after her dream of being a novelist. In support of that dream, she has been taking writing classes and is active in the Midwest Fiction Writers group. And, of course, she sits at her computer and writes. Last fall, she did something else that she'd been wanting to do for a long time: she took a mosaic class.

In many ways, the process of writing is a lot like doing mosaic. You start with the general idea and lay down words one at a time, making changes as you go. Doing mosaic work is, however, a far slower process. Once Georgia began working on her mosaic creations she discovered that her writing output accelerated. Writing came more easily.

## Crosstrain Your Brain

Georgia's not the only person to discover that diverse creative activities can feed one another. Filmmaker Woody Allen plays clarinet in jazz clubs. Paul McCartney paints and writes poetry. Madonna is working on a series of children's books. Not everyone is so willing to look outside their primary field of work to fan their creative spirit.

Maybe it's the old Protestant Work Ethic or maybe it's the

conditioning of our culture that's drilled into us the necessity of focusing on a single occupation. Perhaps it's the fear of doing something badly. Whatever the reason, we're short-changing ourselves if we don't regularly engage in creative crosstraining.

## Creativity Can Be Contagious

One simple way to start taking advantage of this phenomenon is to expose yourself to other people's passions. The world is full of people who are crazy about things you know nothing about.

Last Thanksgiving, I had dinner with a group of distant relatives that I didn't know very well. The sister of the hostess sat next to me at dinner and the moment she sat down said to me, "I would love to have my own business." (Obviously she knew more about me than I did about her!) I asked her if she knew what she wanted to do and she lit right up. "I just love doing beadwork. I come home from my job and go right to my project room and bead all night." The moment dinner was over, she whipped out her beads and spent the afternoon making jewelry. It was fascinating to watch her work and her enthusiasm was utterly contagious.

A few minutes later, my cousin Ray came over to visit with me. Ray has been a farmer his entire life raising corn and soy-beans. Two years ago, he turned several acres of his farm into vineyards—a rather unusual crop in our part of the world. Although he doesn't make wine himself, he grows the grapes for a vintner. In Ray's second year of production, his crop outperformed all expectations. He was so excited about this new aspect of his business—and had a list of ideas he wanted to try—that I wanted to learn more. I promised to return to see the vineyards in the summer.

Although I may never take up beading or growing grapes myself, being with these passionate folks opened a creative valve in me. I spent the long drive home stopping frequently to jot down ideas for my own business.

## Broaden Your Creative Horizons

"Good for the body is the work of the body, and good for the soul is the work of the soul, and good for either is the work of the other," said Henry David Thoreau. No wonder those folks who lived through the Italian Renaissance accomplished so much. I always think that their unspoken motto was something like, "Make love. Make art. Make music. Make business. Make a difference." There's much to learn from that example.

If you're in need of a creative lift—or want to accelerate your output—consider taking up a new pursuit that requires using some dormant creative muscles. Find a class. Hire a coach. Buy a video. Apprentice yourself. Don't worry about whether or not you'll make money from it. That's not the point here. Just taking up a new activity will rejuvenate the more familiar things you're doing. It's that kind of engagement in multiple creative pursuits that is leading more and more of us to think of ourselves not as businesspeople but as creators who just happen to do business.

*To Affirm:* Creative crosstraining is a valuable part of my overall fitness plans.

*To Consider:* Do you have diverse creative interests? Have you had the experience of having one creative activity impact another in a positive way? Is there a creative activity that's been calling to you? Maybe it's time to answer.

# If You Want to Change the World

*The moment you enter the world of business you will have a hundred opportunities a day to act beneficially or wrongly, to deal with people fairly or otherwise, to enhance your social environment or pollute it.*
Paul Hawken

A wave of evangelistic fervor swept across the world in the sixties as political and social activists picked up their placards and took to the street trying to rally support for the cause *du jour*. Eventually, public protests dwindled to occasional events. A sign of indifference and apathy? Maybe not. More likely, protesters discovered that public protests were not particularly effective.

Nevertheless, change is the one constant in our world. Like it or not, we are now living in the time that trendspotter Faith Popcorn predicted would see more change than any in history. Bill Gates predicts the next ten years will bring more change than we've seen in the past thirty. Changing times are often chaotic times causing people to feel confused and powerless. But those who understand and embrace change are often those who make the grandest contribution.

## The Inner Game
If you'd like to change the world or change your life or even a tiny aspect of either, it's important to understand the Inner Game of Making Change. Even though we think of activism as

taking outward actions, the truth is that it's impossible to do so effectively if we don't make the inner change that needs to precede it. Change, whether sweeping or small, may have an outside catalyst but the real thing is always an inside job.

For starters, realize that change comes in two different packages and you need to tell them apart. There's Imposed Change which is the kind we can do little about. Taxes get raised, fashion designers insist we stop wearing willow green or road construction makes travel difficult. We have to make peace with Imposed Change in our own way.

Then there's Instigated Change. That's the kind we think of as improving our lives because we have chosen it. Instigated Change is also preceded by inner change which raises our awareness prior to taking action. It's important to understand this if improvement is to come about.

## Being a Change Agent

Whether we've enlisted or not, the moment we start a business, we also volunteer to be an agent of change. There are several operating philosophies held by those who are successful change agents. Great entrepreneurs share these philosophies with social activists:

No One Is Coming To Save Me—"I was always waiting around for someone to fix the world," confessed singer John Denver. "And then I realized that if the world was going to work, it was up to me." This is the jumping off point for self-liberation.

I Can't Change It All By Myself—Some of us are under the

delusion that we must do it all and do it now. As Stephen Covey points out so eloquently, effective people focus their energy and effort on what he calls our Circle of Influence—the places where our actions can make a difference. In so doing that Circle expands and we become even more powerful and effective. That expansion begins with what the Serenity Prayer calls the wisdom to know the difference between what can and cannot be changed.

My Responsibility Is To Do What I Can Where I Am— Gandhi's admonition to "Be the change you want to see happen in the world," is perhaps the wisest advice on creating change. We must model change—not try to impose it. Diane Pike, a spiritual writer and teacher, talks about her days as an activist in the Peace Movement. One day she realized the hypocrisy of her actions, admitting that it was foolish to scream about peace on earth when she hadn't created peace within herself.

## Business Can Be an Agent of Change

All three of those principles can be beautifully expressed through running a business. By our very nature, inspired entrepreneurs want to leave the world better than we found it. By taking responsibility to positively impact the lives of everyone touched by our businesses (which often draws us out into a bigger playground) we see our own Circles of Influence grow. Without even realizing it, we become role models of a healthier way to live and be in the world. We work to solve problems, not just complain about them. We may even discover that we're pioneering a social change that will make it possible for those coming along behind us to more easily share their creative visions with the rest of us.

That may sound like a tall order for a little business but it's happening every day wherever the entrepreneurial spirit shines. Isn't that more exciting than spending life in a cubicle?

*To Affirm:* I work daily to make my business an agent of positive change.

*To Consider:* Have your ideas about how to instigate change evolved over time? Have you been frustrated by trying to make change and seeing poor results? When have you known that you were being an effective change agent?

# On Being Accountable

*Good character is more to be praised than outstanding talent. Most talents are, to some extent, a gift. Good character, by contrast, is not given to us. We have to build it piece by piece—by thought, choice, courage and determination.*
John Luther

The best thing about being self-employed is that there aren't any timeclocks, performance reviews or limited vacations. The worst thing about being self-employed is that there aren't any timeclocks, performance reviews or limited vacations. Without the deadlines and expectations of others, many would-be entrepreneurs flounder.

It's not just the headiness of all that time we have to manage for ourselves. Distractions, isolation and lack of clarity can all conspire to keep us from growing the business of our dreams. If you are flawlessly disciplined and set deadlines which you unfailingly meet, this essay is not for you. On the other hand, if you suspect that there's room for improvement, that you could accomplish more in a week than is now evident, then I'm talking to you.

## Choose to be Accountable

This past year, I've worked with three webmasters. Not only do they all live in different places, they all have different styles of working. Two of them respond quickly and helpfully to every request I make of them. The third one does not share their urgency. I've come to learn that he'll get things done but he operates in a time frame that I can't comprehend. Hardly a day passes when I don't think about replacing him ... and may have done so by the time you read this.

I don't think being accountable is an accident. It's a discipline that we need to embrace if we are to have colleagues and clients who know they can depend on us to do what we say we're going to do. It's a hard discipline to master if you're devoted to pleasing others at the expense of yourself.

## Learn to Say No

This is a lesson almost every entrepreneur learns the hard way. When our business is young, we're so thrilled that anyone wants to do business with us that we agree to all sorts of things that would have been wiser to pass by. When we say yes and want to say no, we end up making excuses and apologizing for things that couldn't possibly get done.

In Mark Forster's terrific book, *Get Everything Done and Still Have Time to Play*, he writes extensively about the importance of learning to say no. He also recommends that we learn to say no in a neutral tone of voice. He writes, "Never sound annoyed, shamefaced or harassed. Say something along the lines of 'I appreciate you asking me but I can't fit it into my priorities at the moment.' Don't elaborate." You can do that, can't you?

## Have Back-up

Barbara Sher points out that since the Stone Age things have gotten done because of the power of the group. Being accountable to others who want us to succeed can be enormously effective.

Paul McCartney once told an interviewer that he used to drive his late wife Linda to cooking classes. The first week, he went to a back room and spent the time writing a song. When the class ended, people asked McCartney if he hadn't been bored waiting. "No," he said. "I wrote this little tune. Would you like to hear it?" The class was thrilled, of course, to be the first to listen to a new creation and it became his weekly ritual. Knowing they were expecting a new song by the end of the class kept him on his toes.

Nick Williams and I have realized that since we've known each other our friendship has had a positive impact on our individual productivity. In a recent conversation we recorded, I mentioned that although we'd never demanded it of each other, that I felt accountable to our relationship and would feel I wasn't doing my part if every time we talked I'd say, "Oh, I haven't been doing much."

Let someone you trust know what you're working on and let them help you stay on track. This isn't the same thing as hiring a professional nag, by the way. We all need someone in our lives that isn't willing to let us settle for less than the best we can be. Finding an entrepreneurial friend can be one of the best things you can do for your business and your mental health.

As Goethe said, "To know someone, here or there, with whom there is understanding—despite distances or thoughts unexpressed—that can make this Earth a garden."

## ON BEING ACCOUNTABLE

*To Affirm:* I am committed to being accountable to my dreams.

*To Consider:* Have you had experiences in your business working with others who weren't accountable? Was it costly in any way? How do you stay on track?

# The Gift of Delay

*God's delays are not God's denials.*
Robert Schuller

One of the things I love most about traveling is that it can be a metaphor for the rest of our lives. Outside of familiar surroundings, we are apt to be more alert, more conscious. In such situations, we frequently gain new insights into our behavior ... like learning how we respond to unexpected delays and detours.

## The Best Laid Plans

After spending ten days with my siblings in Lucca, Italy, I planned to take the train back to Venice, have a bonus afternoon in my favorite city, then fly home the next day. That plan began to unravel when I went to buy my train ticket and discovered a 24-hour strike was scheduled for exactly the time I wanted to travel. After making numerous telephone calls to find an alternative option, I was assured that some trains would still be running. What I wasn't told was that I'd be making a five-hour sidetrip to Bologna. That little surprise didn't arrive until we'd all gotten off the train in Bologna. Many of my fellow travelers were visibly upset.

Realizing there was nothing I could do about the change in plans, I decided to look for the gift in this delay. I also suspected I was being naively optimistic. Nevertheless, I attached myself to the Del Prado family from the Philippines who were back-packing around Europe with their five delightful children. Wing, the mother, was not coping with the delay very well so I invited her to have a cappuccino with me. When I answered her question about what I do, she said, "You're talking about me!" I spent the next several minutes learning about her business selling hand-made children's clothing. Then I chatted with the eldest son, Ramon, who has started a business as an animator and is about to have his first film shown on television.

While getting to know these entrepreneurial folks was great fun, the thing that everyone noticed about the Del Prados was how kind the children were to each other. That same kindness was extended to me and when we finally parted at the train station in Venice, we were all on the verge of tears. The father said, "Thank you for making our trip so pleasant. We'll think of you as Auntie Barbara."

As I walked off into the darkness toward my hotel, I immediately noticed the sidewalk was covered with water and raised platforms had been brought in to make walking possible. When I got to the hotel, I asked about the flooding and was told there'd been such a storm all day in Venice that it looked like a hurricane was coming through. Had I arrived at the time I wanted to, I'd have gotten drenched and had to spend the afternoon and evening in my hotel room. Meeting the Del Prados was a lot more fun than that.

## So Where's the Gift?

Do you have a project that appears to be delayed? Is success arriving more slowly than you'd expected? Are you thinking of abandoning your great idea? Perhaps you need to slow down a minute, let go a lot and take another look at what's happening.

While deadlines are sometimes necessary, we humans also fool ourselves into thinking we can predict with absolute certainty how long things need to take. But how can you possibly know the length of time involved in doing something you've never done before? How can you know what variables are at play?

When things aren't happening as rapidly as you'd like, start looking for the gift in the delay. Perhaps you need time to develop skills for handling new levels of success with grace. Or maybe your ideas are just a bit ahead of the market and you have to wait for it to catch up with your new vision. Or possibly what looks like a delay is actually an opportunity to receive something bigger and better than you originally desired.

## Keep Going Anyway

President Calvin Coolidge wrote these famous words which are as true today as when he first shared them: "Nothing will take the place of persistence. Talent will not; nothing is more common than unsuccessful people with talent. Genius will not; unrewarded genius is almost a proverb. Education will not; the world is full of educated derelicts. Persistence and determination are omnipotent. The slogan 'Press on' has solved and will always solve the problems of the human race."

*To Affirm:* I actively seek the gift in every delay.

*To Consider:* When has a delay served you well? Are you more apt to allow impatience to frustrate and stop you? Has asking for help ever gotten you past a delay?

# Overcoming Inertia

*Even if you're on the right track, you'll get run over if you just sit there.*
Will Rogers

It's no secret that people who lead rich, satisfying lives think and behave differently from those who do not. What does seem to be a secret is that the more successful among us focus on concepts and let their imaginations work out the form. Looking back over a long, creative life, Buckminster Fuller confessed, "I didn't start out to design a house on a pole or a three-wheeled car. My objective has been humanity's comprehensive welfare in the universe. I could have ended up with a pair of flying slippers."

As Fuller and all great achievers discovered, the first rule of success is to put yourself into the game. The real enemy of success, after all, isn't failure: it's inertia.

## Stretch Farther

There's no one more exciting to be around than someone actively engaged with an idea that delights them. Joanne Collins is a designer of glassware, dinnerware and textiles who radiates enthusiasm. On a flight to Europe she decided to reinvent her business. That decision led her to hire a tutor to help her master Adobe Photoshop. "Now I wake up in the middle of the night," she says, "with all sorts of new ideas. Sometimes I can see how I can rework old designs. Now instead of painting a single dish, I am thinking, 'This could be a collection.'" Collins is a vivid reminder that when we stretch farther, we can't go back.

How can you generate more ideas and action of your own? Quite simply, begin by avoiding idea-dampening situations and embrace wild possibilities instead. The creative process requires a welcoming environment and shuns those who refuse to pay attention. Know who and what inspires you and make that your natural habitat.

## Another Inertia-busting Concept

Rigid routine is the enemy of creativity. In the name of efficiency, many people set up their lives so they do the same things at the same time with the same people day in and day out. It's not surprising that Joanne Collins' big idea came to her during a flight; many people report that a change of scenery opens their minds to thoughts they hadn't had before. In order to take advantage of this stimulus, stir things up frequently.

## And Another

Be an enthusiastic problem solver. Many folks live in a perpetual state of problem-avoidance, treating problems as punishment. Yet the seed of real opportunity almost always arrives dressed as a problem in need of a solution.

Another great way to postpone success is to focus on nonexistent problems, rather than solving the ones that represent taking the next step. I once met a woman who told me that she was launching a singing career and had just recorded her first album. However, she was consumed by the fact that she also had a chronic illness and now fretted that should her career take off she'd be unable to travel. She was busy trying to solve a problem that she didn't yet have. I hear variations of that all the time. That's not prudence; it's procrastination. Knowing that you're a champion problem solver is an enormous confidence builder and an open invitation for ideas to plant themselves in your patch.

## Don't Think So Much

Inertia also can be caused by thinking too much. True success is a heart game more than a head game. Our minds, which are so necessary in many ways, can also harbor self-doubt and destruction. For many people, being alone with their thoughts puts them in enemy territory. Make your mind a friendly place to be.

Years ago, when I was fussing about earthquakes or some such calamity, my sister Margaret calmly pointed out that no matter what the disaster, the odds were always in my favor. I can't begin to count the number of times that bit of wisdom has kept me serene.

Now carry that thought a bit further. If the odds are in our favor in times of disaster, how much more in our favor are they when we're following the prompting of our hearts and souls?

Dreams are fragile things, after all, but as Richard Bach wisely pointed out, "We are never given a dream without also being given the power to make it come true." So put yourself in the game. Trust yourself and value your ideas. Don't hide out from problems and don't bother yourself with imaginary ones. Those are odds that can make things happen. I'd bet on it.

*To Affirm:* Action is the perfect cure for inertia.

*To Consider:* Inertia can often be overcome by very small actions. How can you shake up a routine and get moving on a bigger dream? If you find yourself stuck, assume a different point of view.

# A Foolproof Investment

*I've learned that following what you love magnifies your
talent. You just have to have the faith to invest in it.*
Leslie Rector

Every day we are inundated with advertising that urges us to
buy things that may or may not improve the quality of our
lives. Seldom are we encouraged to invest in experiences that
will enlarge our inner selves.

One day I got a call from a stockbroker who said, "How
would you like to get a higher yield on your investments?"
When I told him that my primary investments were my
businesses, he said, "Oh, isn't that scary?" "Not at all," I said,
"but giving my money to a stranger over the phone is truly
scary."

## What Investing is About

My dictionary defines "invest" this way: to spend money or time
or effort on something that will bring a profit. To invest implies
that you must first put something in, in order to get something
greater out. When most people think about investing, it
generally involves putting money into something rather cold or
impersonal, then waiting in the hope that the investment will
grow. This common practice has a huge element of risk involved
which may be why so many traditional investors stay removed
and uninvolved.

167

## What Investing Could Be About

On the other hand, there's a far lower risk to be had when we invest our money, time and effort in ourselves and our dreams. Although it can be a far better investment to do so, many people have a hard time understanding its importance.

Writer Sondra Ray confronts this attitude. She writes, "Let's take a look at the priorities on which people spend their money. What comes first? The rent; and this is the worst investment on the list. Compare rent with self-improvement. The fact is that self-improvement is the most valuable item on the list and most people don't even have a category for it. Fear of running out causes you to spend only on things people told you to spend money on. When it comes to buying things that are really good for you and that make you happy, guilt comes. When you say, 'I don't have enough money to go to that self-improvement seminar or buy that self-improvement book,' it is almost like saying, 'I am not a good investment.' The best way to make money is to invest in yourself and that is what self-improvement is all about."

When you invest in yourself and your dreams you are making the most important financial decision of your life. You have also invested in the one thing that lasts a lifetime and cannot be taken away from you. The ups and downs of the economy have no effect on your investment in yourself. In fact, if you do it whole-heartedly, you'll acquire skills and tools for circumventing difficult economies.

## Invest in Yourself

Author Jim Rohn has some other suggestions about sound

investing. "Each month," he suggests, "set aside a portion of your income and invest it in your search for knowledge. Spend the money to cultivate the sleeping giant inside you. The money—that's a small price. There can be a great deal of difference between cost and value. I used to ask, 'How much does it cost?' I've learned to ask, 'What is it worth?' When I started to base my life on value instead of price, all kinds of things began to happen. Missing skills, missing knowledge, missing insight, missing values, missing lifestyle are all a result of not reading books or spending time in seminars or with those who have something to teach you.

"The promise is unlimited potential. More important than money is your next expenditure: time. Alas, there are no short-cuts. Until such time that a machine can be hooked up to pour knowledge into the brain, it will take time—precious time. Fortunately, life has a unique way of rewarding high investment with high return. The investment of time you make now may be the catalyst for major accomplishment.

"Finally, you'll be making an investment of effort. There is a great deal more involved in serious learning than in casual learning. In everything you do, be it self-observation, reading or observing others, the intensity of your efforts will have a profound effect on the amount of knowledge you gain. It is precisely this effort that will open the floodgates to the place where great ideas can work their magic."

*To Affirm:* Every investment I make in myself brings a fabulous return.

*To Consider:* In what ways do you invest in yourself now? Have you been stingy or generous in spending time and money and effort to build your best self? What have you done so far that has brought the biggest return on investment?

# Delightfully Surprising Success

*Nothing is impossible; there are ways that lead to everything, and if we had sufficient will, we should always have sufficient means.*
Francois de La Rochefoucauld

Throughout history monasteries and convents have supported themselves in entrepreneurial ways. Making wine, baking bread and offering hospitality to travelers have been popular money-makers. Now there's a new twist: modern monks are expanding their horizons by using technology to create global businesses. In some cases, the results have been nothing short of miraculous.

In rural Wisconsin, six Cistercian monks have demonstrated that the practical and spiritual can combine to build astonishing success. When the monks were horrified by the expense of buying printer supplies, they decided to create their own computer printer inks and offer them to the public. Laser Monks, begun in 2001, grossed a meager $2000 the first year. This year, they're on track to do between $2 and $3 million. (If you go to their Web site, you'll probably want to become a customer too.) Not only do they save their customers enormous sums of money, they'll gladly pray for your business at the same time. What other office supply business offers such a service?

**Fire and Ice**
When you think of ice sculpting (which you probably don't

think about on a regular basis), a great business idea may not be your first response. Don't tell that to the three guys who own Fear No Ice, the only performance ice sculpting company in the world. The idea for this business came about when Scott Rella and his two partners, all chefs, realized that whenever they were sculpting ice for an event, it drew a crowd. Rella says, "I don't know exactly when the moment was but we started saying, 'Instead of just sculpting, why don't we put on a little show?' Now we have our own soundtrack, our own video art and really cool costumes."

Besides performing at the Winter Olympics, Fear No Ice travels the world turning tons of ice into beautiful sculptures. They've even produced pieces of ice art for movie sets and for winter festivals around the world. Their stage show draws large crowds in Las Vegas and everywhere else they perform.

## An Unlikely Hot Title

While we all use (and are confused by) punctuation, that's no predictor of best selling success; but that is, of course, what happened with the enormously popular *Eats, Shoots & Leaves*. Author Lynne Truss is as surprised as anyone that her little treatise on proper placement of apostrophes and commas has taken the publishing world by storm. She writes, "To be clear, no one involved in the production of *Eats, Shoots & Leaves* expected the words 'runaway' and 'bestseller' would ever be associated with it." Yet there it sat atop the bestseller list urging all of us sticklers to unite. Whether or not correct punctuation will become the norm again still remains to be seen.

## What's Their Secret?

No conventional book of business advice would suggest that the road to success is paved with monastic vows, ice sculpting or punctuation instruction. Yet, as is so often the case (thank goodness), conventional wisdom would be wrong. (You have no idea how long I dithered over the placement of that last comma.)

Although these surprise success stories seem to have little in common other than the uniqueness of each enterprise, there is one thing shared in each of these tales: pure unadulterated passion. Yes, even the monks. That passion is underlined by more than a little dose of whimsy and a big dose of creativity. Making a fortune was probably not on the To Do List of any of these entrepreneurs.

And yet, uncommon success may not be so uncommon after all. Nearly every day brings another story of success that no one predicted. Who was telepathic enough to predict that a series of books about a boy wizard would set publishing records worldwide? Certainly not J.K. Rowling who said, "I never set out to make a mark. I set out to do the thing I love best in the world and find out whether I was any good at it."

Whether it's passion for the game of business, an idea, a better way of doing things, personal freedom or living an adventurous life, passion is the thread that runs through every great story of success. "Only passions, great passions, can elevate the mind to great things," said Denis Diderot. Passion unlocks our imaginations and makes us irresistible.

Happily, passion is a renewable resource so if yours has

dwindled or is still buried, make uncovering, reviving and employing yours the highest priority. You just might end up in the Surprising Success Hall of Fame.

*To Affirm:* I allow passion to guide me to surprising success.

*To Consider:* Heard any good stories about surprising success? I even keep a file called You Could Never Make a Living Doing That to gather real-life tales of people who succeeded by listening to their passion. These uncommon folks make great role models.

# Starting Small, Dreaming Big

*When you build a dream, the dream builds you.*
Robert Schuller

Twenty years ago, a scruffy band of street performers began attracting crowds in Quebec, Canada. They're still attracting crowds and, two decades later, more than 40 million people have been dazzled by the imagination and magic of Cirque du Soleil.

During their existence, Cirque has become synonymous with creative performances that cause blasé adults to return to childhood wonder. Every aspect of their performance is extraordinary. Costumes, original music, and sets all add to the spectacle of astonishing acrobatics. Unlike conventional circuses, this one has no animals and each show is organized around a story or theme. Whether they're performing in a tent or a theater, Cirque du Soleil exists to amaze.

Behind all this theater is a business that has grown and evolved as the vision of their founders has taken form. How can these entrepreneurial artists teach us to be more artistic entrepreneurs? After all, their success demonstrates that it isn't just about flying through the air.

## The Vision Thing

A successful entrepreneur from Texas told a reporter, "If you've got an itty-bitty vision, you're going to have an itty-bitty vision." Obviously, Cirque's vision went beyond their original street corner. According to their mission statement, "Cirque du Soleil is dedicated to the creation, production and performance of artistic works whose mission is to invoke, provoke and evoke the imagination, the senses and the emotions of people around the world."

They also have clearly articulated values—also posted on their Web site.

"At Cirque du Soleil we aspire:

- to uphold the integrity of the creative process
- to recognize and respect each individual's contribution to our body of work
- to extend the limits of the possible
- to draw inspiration from our artistic and cultural diversity
- to encourage and promote the potential of youth

When vision and values are shared, it brings alignment and congruity to the effort. Although nearly 3,000 people are now involved in the work of Cirque du Soleil worldwide, this common statement of purpose holds the wildly creative business together.


## Big Dreams Attract

While many people are afraid to dream big, falsely believing it's an invitation to disappointment, making little plans is the real disappointer. "Our prayers are answered," said Morris Adler, "not when we are given what we ask, but when we are challenged to be what we can be."

The big dream that continues to grow through Cirque is

powerfully magnetic. One of their resident shows, *O* at the Bellagio in Las Vegas, has sold out its two nightly performances since it opened over ten years ago. Every year, thousands of gymnasts (many of them former Olympians), performers and musicians from around the world audition for Cirque du Soleil. In fact, Cirque is comprised of artists and employees from over forty countries, speaking twenty-five different languages.

## Willingness

In an introductory talk to a new Cirque troupe, their manager told them, "We are not going to avoid complexity. We are going to operate without clarity. If you need life to be simple you won't like being in Cirque." This willingness to do whatever it takes to create something extraordinary underlines the activities of every outstanding success. Over the years, those who have studied successful people have discovered that winners are willing to do things that the less successful avoid. Usually that willingness begins with starting wherever you are—performing on the street, if necessary.

In our businesses, that might translate to a willingness to do both mundane and lofty chores. It undoubtedly means being willing to do things over and over again with a desire to improve our performance with each repetition. It means not taking the easy way out when the more challenging way confronts us.

## Meeting the Challenge

Today, Cirque du Soleil says its challenge is to continue growing at a sustainable pace "while offering its creators the freedom to dream the wildest dreams and make them come true." Like the most interesting enterprises, Cirque is the place where creativity meets commerce. Both sides of the equation are needed to produce the expanding products and productions that bear the Cirque imprint.

"We grow great by dreams," said Woodrow Wilson. "Some of us let these great dreams die but others nourish and protect them; nurse them through bad days till they bring them to the sunshine and light which comes always to those who sincerely hope that their dreams will come true." Lucky for us that Cirque du Soleil kept their dreams alive and in doing so remind us all to nourish and protect the dreams that are ours.

*To Affirm:* I honor and nurture my wildest dreams.

*To Consider:* How do creativity and commerce co-exist in your business? Do you favor one over the other? Do you find it hard to be artistic and entrepreneurial at the same time?

# Flying Lessons

*You've got to jump off cliffs all the time and build your wings on the way down.*
Ray Bradbury

When Jonathan Livingston Seagull discovers that he can soar, his first impulse is to share this glorious news with his fellow seagulls. Most gulls, he sadly realizes, spend their entire lives going from shore to food and back again. Naturally, they'll be wildly excited to learn that there's so much more they can do!

When Jonathan swoops down with his breathless announcement, he's greeted with total disinterest and feels as if he's flown into a brick-hard wall of resistance. It's a situation familiar to anyone who has chosen to fly higher. Just getting by seems to be the highest aspiration of the majority of folks.

In order to create the life and business of our dreams, we must be willing to do more than go from shore to food and back again. We need to learn to soar. Happily, we can create our own flying lessons and design our own curriculum that will stretch us in new directions. It may come as a surprise to learn that our flying begins with several earthbound activities.

## Plant Yourself in a Fertile Environment
Identifying what you want to do is only a tiny first step. You must then place yourself in situations that support your success. That means finding others who can nurture and teach you.

In his mind-opening book, *The Little Money Bible*, Stuart Wilde talks about closing the gap between where you are and where you want to be. Sometimes it's a matter of physical distance, he says. "Closing the physical distance is a matter of showing up in the marketplace, becoming a face that people know, demonstrating your expertise and getting into the loop where the movers and shakers are. People who could bestow great opportunities upon you aren't scouring the distant hills for talent. They're in the flow." Don't plant your dreams—or yourself—in a desert and expect to see growth.

## Do Something Difficult

When my sisters, brother and I were in Italy, I asked my brother Jim how he managed to stay so fit. After he explained his eating and exercising routines, he said something I've never heard another person say: "And I try to do something hard everyday."

Purposely doing the difficult is not only good for physical fitness. It's also a way to build character and many other fine qualities we find in life's winners. The key here is to keep finding new ways to challenge yourself since most things which are difficult become easy after repeated encounters.

## Be an Instigator

While assuming a leadership role seems risky for many people, it's often the most expedient way to advance a dream or create a growth-supporting environment. It's a concept understood by a woman I know named Grace who sent out an invitation that read: "ART NIGHTS AT GRACE'S. Play with your friends.

Bring your art project du jour. Start something new. Experiment. Make a big fat mess. Lose track of time. Sink into an atmosphere of encouragement. Prime the pump. Get the juices flowing. Do nothing. Wing it. Every third Wednesday evening at Grace's place." Waiting for things to happen is not the way to fly; making things happen is.

## Build an Option Bank

An Option Bank, just like the place where you store money, is a repository of good ideas, dreams and goals. And like an ordinary bank, the more you put in, the more you can draw out. The best way to get started at this is by realizing that there is never just a single option available to you. If you begin with that premise, your creative spirit will be on alert and start going to work scanning for possibilities. On the other hand, if you are stuck and believe that your only way out is closed for repairs, your life will begin to shrink, not expand.

Of all the wise things said by designer Coco Chanel, my favorite is this: "If you were born without wings, do nothing to prevent their growing." Why not make this a time to grow wider wings? Like Jonathan Livingston Seagull, you'll soon discover that the gull who flies highest sees farthest.

*To Affirm:* I find numerous ways to grow wings on my dreams.

*To Consider:* In which of these four flying lessons are you the strongest? What, exactly, have you done to build that strength? Do you ever purposely do something difficult?

# Language Matters

*Remember that you are a human being with a soul and the divine gift of articulate speech—that your native language is the language of Shakespeare and Milton and the Bible— so don't sit there crooning like a bilious pigeon.*
Professor Henry Higgins

We are living in the Information Age where words are the tools we wield but even bright and educated people don't always realize why language is important. A friend and I were having dinner one night when I mentioned that I was appalled to hear the flight attendant on my regular airline announce at the end of the flight, "Have a nice day wherever your destination takes you."

My friend shrugged. "Doesn't matter to me," she said. "Oh, but it does matter," I said. "If they're careless with their public communication, maybe they're careless with other things—like maintenance." My friend remained unconvinced and that's a shame because it's only when we realize the extraordinary power of words that we begin to use them purposefully. In the end, eloquence isn't so much a talent as it is the result of fascination with word power.

## Positive or Negative?
You don't have to look very far to find people who fill the world with negative thoughts converted into negative words. There

was a popular bumper sticker that declared, "I owe, I owe. So off to work I go." Apparently that dismal sentiment captured the fancy of the owner of a sports car who has a vanity plate that reads IOIO. Imagine having that affirmation of indebtedness being constantly reinforced.

On the other hand, word power is one of the most available and accessible tools we have to use as entrepreneurs. Consider, for example, the importance of choosing the right words to describe yourself and your business. We become even more aware of the importance of words when it's time to name a product or service.

A few years ago, the University of Minnesota Extension Service decided to offer a seminar called "Transferring Non-Title Property," a title that was factual but hardly catchy. The perfect title presented itself one day when one of the planners shared a personal experience. Out of that came the seminar title, "Who Gets Grandma's Yellow Pie Plate?" That perfect choice of words has drawn more than 20,000 people to the seminar.

## Simple Tools for Better Expression

Whether you desire genuine eloquence or hardly give language a thought, here are four simple steps that can improve personal self-expression.

Listen to Yourself. In ordinary conversation, most of us don't hear ourselves because we're so busy thinking about what is being said or what we're going to say when it's our turn. Make an effort to listen. Become aware of your style, your vocabulary, your ability to put ideas into words. A session with your tape recorder can help you hear the sound of your voice and make you aware of changes you may want to master.

Build Your Vocabulary. One study of successful people found that the only common denominator among them was a large vocabulary. Not adding words to your vocabulary is like keeping the same wardrobe for your entire life. When you encounter a new word, don't let it slip by. Grab your dictionary. And read your dictionary just for fun, too. As writer Hart Crane observed, "One must be drenched in words, literally soaked in them, to have the right ones form themselves into the proper pattern at the right moment."

Get Rid of Obscenities. I was once invited to lunch by a woman I'd never met. Throughout our time together, she used expletives and vulgar expressions with amazing ease. While I'm not prudish about profanity (and believe it serves a useful purpose when used sparingly and appropriately), I'm always surprised when a total stranger casually uses obscenities. If you're going to use four-letter words, you need to know your audience.

Learn to Edit. "He that uses many words for the explaining of any subject," wrote John Ray, "doth, like the cuttlefish, hide himself for the most part in his own ink." Editing is the process of removing the unnecessary so what remains has impact. Masterful communicators cut to the bone. Fuzzy communicators can't distinguish between the important and the unimportant so they say everything—hoping to cover all bases, I guess. Eliminate verbosity and dazzle people with precision.

**It's Worth the Bother**

While nobody communicates perfectly all the time, aiming at mastery in using words is both a fascinating pastime and an amazing confidence builder.

And what's the payoff? It may be bigger than you realize. Consider what Lord Byron wrote long before the age of mass communication:

> But words are things, and a small drop of ink
> Falling like dew, upon a thought, produces
> That which makes thousands, perhaps millions,
> think.

*To Affirm:* My capacity for communication gets better with every passing day.

*To Consider:* I'm fascinated by titles of books, seminars, etc. as well as the names people give their businesses. Do you know of any examples of someone who changed a ho-hum title or name into an attention-getter? Have you had a personal experience of finding just the right words and producing better results because of them?

# Willing to be Inspired

*Be with those who help your being.*
Rumi

It was years ago when I stumbled across Helene Hanff's *84, Charing Cross Road* on the shelves of the public library. The book is a collection of letters written between Hanff, a struggling New York writer and passionate booklover, and the manager of a London bookshop from whom she ordered books. As time went on, the letters became more personal as the two correspondents became great friends.

I adored the book, although it was a long time before I found out that the story didn't end there. When Hanff learned that her friend had died, she gathered up their letters, thinking they might make an interesting magazine article. Eventually, a publisher saw her manuscript and suggested the letters be turned into a book. Not only did the book receive rave reviews, it became a favorite of Anglophiles and bibliophiles everywhere. A few years later, the story was made into a BBC production, then a stage play and, in 1987, a movie starring Anne Bancroft and Anthony Hopkins.

## Life-changing Letters
In her subsequent book, *The Duchess of Bloomsbury Street*, Hanff writes, "I tell you, life is extraordinary. A few years ago I couldn't write anything or sell anything. I'd had my chance and

done my best and failed. And how was I to know the miracle waiting to happen round the corner in late middle age? *84, Charing Cross Road* was no bestseller, you understand; it didn't make me rich or famous. It just got me hundreds of letters and phone calls from people I never knew existed; it got me wonderful reviews; it restored a self-confidence and self-esteem I'd lost somewhere along the way. It brought me to England. It changed my life."

What Hanff's experience so brilliantly illustrates is this: opportunity is not so much a matter of finding the right thing as it is about recognizing the right thing—and acting upon it. How can anyone hear a story like hers and not be inspired by the message of following your own heart?

## Avoiding Inspiration

Lately, I seem to have more than my share of conversations with people who are downright inert. Rather than recognizing the opportunities that are right under their noses, they're waiting for a personal assignment from God or for the Administration to change or for the weather to improve. I've known people who have spent the last ten years—and longer—waiting to get started. These are the people Eric Clapton accuses of squandering their gifts. What is holding them back? When I've come right out and asked that question their replies are always flimsy.

Closer inspection reveals that none of these frustrated souls personally identifies with success. They would never read a Helene Hanff book, for instance, and think, "Wow! That could be me!" In fact, they actively look for ways in which they are unlike winners—perhaps to justify their own lack of achievement.

There's a man who personifies what I'm talking about. This guy is quite smug about the fact that he gets so many terrific ideas, often pointing out, "I'm a real idea person." His friends have been polite enough not to mention that not one of those ideas has ever been acted on. Not long ago, I told him about a mutual friend named Stan who had just received a big grant. Mr. Great Ideas responded by saying Stan was lucky to be in a field that handed out money freely, implying, of course, that he could never be so blessed. In contrast, a woman to whom I told the same story, promptly began investigating grant opportunities for herself.

## Take it Personally

People tell me that they have no role models around them. The truth is, they're just not paying attention. Wonderful stories of success are everywhere, even if we don't personally know the leading character. Just as it is with opportunity, it's not so much a matter of finding role models as it is about recognizing them ... and being smart enough to learn what they have to teach.

*To Affirm:* I am willing to be inspired by the highest and the best.

*To Consider:* While it's quite natural for children to have role models, why do you think it's so rare among adults? Have you got a favorite autobiography that inspired you on first reading it? If so, why did you identify with that person?

# Little Things Mean More Than You May Think

*Incompetence springs from indifference.*
Arnold Glasgow

When I was visiting my daughter in Los Angeles, we kept seeing a vehicle parked in various spots around her neighborhood. This eye-catcher was a dirty and dented white van with huge lettering on the sides that read, "Yoga. First class free." It did not look like it belonged to someone who had found inner peace.

A few evenings later, I saw a story on the local news about the hottest exercise class in town. It, too, was a yoga class but the instructor had added a soothing touch that seemed to magnetize students. The packed studio was lit by candlelight and a string quartet played gentle music as the practitioners went through their poses. Every class was full to overflowing.

These yoga teachers are a vivid reminder that little things can make a huge difference. Happily, those little things are within the reach of all of us, no matter if we're just starting out or if we've got years of experience behind us.

**Five Rules**
Dan Millman, the author of *Way of the Peaceful Warrior* and several other books, says that he has five rules for living and for

189

writing. They are: show up, pay attention, tell your truth, do your best, don't be attached to outcomes. In the context of writing, he explains how he applied these rules through five years of working to get his writing career back on track. He says, "Show up means sitting down in the chair in front of your computer or writing pad. Pay attention means to look, listen, touch, smell, taste life and write for the senses; then read your writing, notice the weaknesses and improve your work. Tell your truth means to write as only you can, for no one else can write exactly as you do. Do your best means constant rewriting until you are certain you cannot improve another sentence. Don't be attached to outcomes means that you cannot control the outcomes, only the effort."

Those rules sound simple but few people seem to apply them to their work. In fact, sloppy workers often dismiss their poor performance by bragging that they're really not into details— as if being concerned with details is beneath them. This attitude carries a heavy penalty since long-term success depends on doing many little things as exquisitely as we can. After all, it's often the details that distinguish us from the competition.

**Avoid This Deception**
People who perform indifferently deceive themselves by thinking that when they're successful or when their screenplay gets filmed or when they lose weight, they'll become pleasant and positive. It doesn't work that way. People who move forward in life don't wait for perfect conditions before making the effort to do their best. And people who don't do their best

with the more mundane and prosaic aspects of their work seldom get the opportunity for grander things.

But getting bigger and better assignments isn't the only—or even the best—reason for doing every task as well as possible. As television mogul Norman Lear points out, "Success is how you collect your minutes. You spend millions of minutes to reach one triumph, one moment, then you spend maybe a thousand minutes enjoying it. If you were unhappy through those millions of minutes, what good are the thousands of minutes of triumph? It doesn't equate."

## Be Creative

Admittedly, it takes character and commitment to smile your way through drudgery but the dullest task can be bearable when it's viewed as a necessary part of a bigger vision. If stuffing a thousand envelopes is part of your marketing plan, for instance, it becomes one facet of sharing your enthusiasm for what your business has to offer. You could even turn that tedious job into a special event like my friend Eugene did when he decided to market the oil from his olive groves. Since having the bottles labeled was too costly for his shoestring budget, he invited willing friends for dinner and an evening of gluing labels on the bottles by hand. Not only did he get the job done, his enthusiasm for his new venture was so contagious that his friends became instant supporters of his success.

So what are you supposed to be doing today? Whatever it is make positive effort for good. What you do today does matter. If your dream seems far, far away, make even stronger effort to move a little bit closer. Unless you wholeheartedly support your dreams with action, how can you expect anyone else to care?

And if you don't know what you are to do next, light candles. Play chamber music. Breathe. Or go wash the van.

*To Affirm:* I invest creativity and enthusiasm in every detail.

*To Consider:* Have you found a way to bring grace and enthusiasm to a small task? Have you discovered you could find pleasure in mundane aspects of your business? What makes the difference in a task being a pleasure or a pain?

# Time to Quit

*Every time I go into the studio I wonder if I can still deliver the goods.*
Madonna

There's a favorite story that I tell in my *Making a Living Without a Job* seminar about Claudia Jessup and Genie Chipps who started a service business in New York called Supergirls. It's a story that first opened my eyes to the possibility of creating a business that was an extension of what I loved to do.

That story assumed another role when I decided that I would know it was time to quit when I walked out of a seminar thinking I couldn't bear to tell the Supergirls story one more time. When we're launching a business, quitting is the farthest thing from our mind. However, people quit projects all the time and often do so from an emotional position, not a rational one. Some people give up at the first sign of a challenge while others hang on long after the joy has ended. So there are times when quitting is the smartest thing to do and other times when it's a sign of weakness. Let's examine the differences.

## Smart to Quit
Years ago Ralph Waldo Emerson pointed out that everything in life has a price and if that price is not paid you'll receive something else, not the thing you desire. Often the price of

success is quitting what you're doing in order to do something else. You may have to quit doing things ineffectively in order to work productively. Or quit watching television to have time to create another profit center. Or stop working for someone else's dream so you can go after your own.

This kind of quitting isn't giving up on your dreams. It's letting go of the lesser so the greater good can happen. When looked at from this position you can see that knowing when to quit is as important as knowing when to start.

So how can you know when it's time to quit? Well, sometimes you just know. There's an internal sense of completion, there's nothing more for you to learn or contribute. It's time to move on to the next challenge.

**Know Your Motivation**
In other situations the decision may not be so obvious. Is quitting a fear choice ( I'm going to fail at this) or a growth choice (I need to expand myself in new ways)? You might also ask yourself if are walking away because you haven't really invested yourself fully in a project.

Then there's the issue of commitment to your vision. Are you willing to be uncomfortable for a while in order to accomplish a long-term goal? Nena and George O'Neill, the authors of *Shifting Gears*, explain what real commitment means. "The difference between conditional commitment and complete commitment is a question of time. With a half-step you say to yourself, 'I'm going to try this for a specific amount of time and see if it works.' With full commitment, you say, 'I'm going to live this way for an indefinite length of time, for as long as I feel happy and fulfilled.'" It is possible to be uncomfortable and happy at the same time. Only you can decide if your current dreams are worthy of your commitment. If not, quitting may be in order—and soon.

**Another Option**

I see many people who think they've failed when the truth is that that just ran out of patience and imagination. Maybe, rather than quitting altogether, you just need to redesign what you're doing. For two years, John Schroeder and Shane Groth published a newsletter called *Church Ideas*. When they decided not to continue with the publication, they realized that they had a superb collection of articles and information. They gathered up what they had produced, submitted it to a publisher and the result was *The Church Ideabook*, the first of several books they co-authored.

**Choose and Choose Again**

Life constantly asks us to make choices. You can't be dependent and independent at the same time ... or decisive and indecisive. That's the good news. We can always rethink the choices we've made and give up the ones that aren't moving us forward. Loudon Wainwright said, "Perhaps the best reason for having calendars and for marking life in years is that the cycle itself offers hope. We need fresh starts and new chances, the conviction that beginnings remain available, no matter how many we've blown. And the yearly clock can start anywhere along the line."

But you might have to quit first.

*To Affirm:* I am wise enough to know when it's time to quit and move on.

*To Consider:* Looking at the O'Neill's definition of commitment, in what ways have you made conditional commitments and what ways have you made full commitments? Would you be better off if you quit the conditional situation? Is there a project that is stalled that might benefit from a redesign? Do you believe (secretly or consciously) that it's more noble not to quit—even when all signs point that it's the wisest way?

# Thinking Entrepreneurially

*Owning a business and working for one are as different as chalk and cheese.*
Paul Hawken

For years, Apple Computers has used the slogan Think Different. It's a slogan that describes the entrepreneurial mind as well as this innovative business. Over and over again, I marvel at the differences in the ways that entrepreneurs tackle problems, use their imagination and go after dreams compared to the way non-entrepreneurs go about the same things.

What are the thinking processes that make such a difference? On closer inspection, they're simpler things than you might suppose. That doesn't make them any less powerful, however.

## It Starts With a Vision

One of my new favorite television programs is *Building Character* on the Home and Garden channel. Each episode features three stories about people who have taken old buildings—like a fortune cookie factory or cheese warehouse—and turned them into unique homes. A common theme seems to run through these renovations. Time after time, the home-owners will say, "Everyone thought I was crazy to think this rundown wreck could be salvaged but I could just see the potential." In most of the stories, the renovation is the first the owner ever tackled. It's obvious that vision compensates for lack of experience.

"Ideas are the beginning points of all fortunes," said Napoleon Hill. "Ideas are the products of the imagination." Successful Dreambuilders see possibilities where others only see current circumstances. Consequently, their efforts are directed towards bringing the vision to life rather than lamenting the problems or difficulties.

## Create Multiple Options

Last year, Valerie Young organized a brilliant retreat for which I was one of the presenters. From the moment she began promoting it through her ezine, she began getting angry e-mails from people complaining about the price. Since the retreat was named *Making Dreams Happen*, I saw getting there as Exercise Number One. When she sent out an SOS to me, I replied by saying, "This is just a simple exercise in goal setting. Why don't we have a contest and see who comes up with the most creative ways of funding the seminar?" Some people got excited at that challenge; others continued to pout.

What a contrast that was to a recent experience I had. Two friends and I decided to make a trip to Las Vegas. Both of them have been working on writing books so neither had much cash flow at the moment. However, once the decision was made, they both swung into action and within a few days had created the money they needed for the trip. Both of them have Option Banks that they can draw on when they want to.

Entrepreneurs decide first what they want to have happen;

then they focus on mobilizing their options to make it happen. Those who don't think entrepreneurially are stuck with limited options and resources.

## Think Different

In late April, *Time* magazine did a special issue naming the 100 most influential people living today. Two that made the list were Sergey Brin and Larry Page, more famously known as The Google Guys. Back in 1997, Brin and Page were working on their PhDs in computer science at Stanford when they figured out how to index and rank websites in the order of how often they were linked to. They were so certain of their idea's merits that they quit school to start a company.

According to *Time*, "Their business naiveté was a plus, helping them avoid many common mistakes of the dotcom age. For instance, the site went live before Page and Brin had thought to hire a webmaster. So while search giants like Yahoo were filling their home pages with news headlines, stock quotes and sports scores, Google had nothing but a search box and log. 'Other companies would boast about how users spent 45 minutes on their sites,' says Page. 'We wanted people to spend a minimum amount of time on Google. The faster they got their results, the more they'd use it.'" Six years later, Google has indexed over 8 billion Web pages, sees 200 million searches every day and has entered the language as a verb.

## It's a Daily Exercise

If you want to stack the odds in your favor, spend time each and every day contemplating your vision, adding another option and thinking more creatively. Even a small amount of time set aside to consciously exercise these techniques will bring a noticeable return on your investment.

*To Affirm:* My daily thoughts are those of a dreambuilding entrepreneur.

*To Consider:* How have you resisted the urge to follow the crowd or conform? Do you find doing so is exciting or does it make you question your sanity? How could you make it easier to live a visionary, option-filled life?

# Disappointing Results

*Talent is long patience.*—Gustav Flaubert

Six thousand people showed up at the Target Center in Minneapolis to hear Sting and Annie Lennox a few weeks ago. The venue holds more than three times that many people. Do you suppose that the performers only gave a third of their usual effort? If you've been in business for a while, you're probably reminded of some down cycles of your own. After all, ebb and flow are part of the entrepreneurial journey but that doesn't mean we're immune from feeling disappointed.

This week I'd like you to consider a slightly radical thought: how you behave during the slow times may affect your long-term success far more than what you do when things are rolling along smoothly. Here are some valuable tools to use when the phone isn't ringing, the crowd at the art fair is half the estimated size or your mailbox is so empty it echoes.

## Commit to Your Commitments

In the early days of building her speaking business, Karyn was scheduled to fly from her home in Denver to Seattle to teach in an adult education program. A few days before her seminar, she got a call from the center saying she only had six students enrolled and she was free to cancel. Karyn said, "No, I won't cancel. If there are six people who want to know about handling stress with humor, I'll be there for them." Even though this meant that Karyn would lose money by keeping her commitment, she went to Seattle and delivered her best program.

As it turned out, one of the participants in her class worked for Microsoft and recognized that Karyn's material would be extremely valuable to that corporation. Several months later, Karyn returned to Seattle to do a program for the software giant which, of course, paid her handsomely.

Knowing Karyn, I also know that she'd have looked for some other hidden benefit in the first small seminar such as seeing this as another chance to polish her performance. Sometimes the biggest reward may simply be the added opportunity to practice and improve. There's always a benefit if you look for it, but only if you treat your personal commitments as important.

## Keep Moving

"Too many people quit before they start," observed the prolific Thomas Edison. When we're not getting the response we want, it can be tempting to call a halt but quiet times should be a call to action, not inactivity.

I often walk in the evening at the Mall of America and notice how many shops are being staffed by a lethargic person glumly sitting behind the counter. I seldom even glance at their merchandise. It's the stores where things are happening that get my attention. Ernest Holmes writes about the phenomenon of activity in *Creative Mind and Success*. He says, "Act as though things were happening even though they may not appear to be. Keep things moving and soon you will have to avoid the rush. Activity is genius. Half the businesses that you go into make you sleepy and you feel as if you can't get out fast enough. The other half are alive and those are the ones who are doing the business of the world."

## Give It Your Best

It's not easy to turn in a superb performance when nobody seems to be watching. Do it anyway.

Not only will you keep getting better and better at what you're doing, you owe it to the people you serve to give them the best you can muster all of the time—even when you wish there were more of them.

Not long ago, Oprah Winfrey enjoyed a sandwich from a small shop in San Luis Obispo, California. When she learned that the owner, Marqaux Sky, was planning to close the business, Oprah decided to invest. She explained her decision to support the struggling entrepreneur by saying, "Always do your best. You never know who's watching." That's a success secret Oprah learned when she was the host of a local talk show in Chicago (not the household name she's become) and Quincy Jones saw her on television and recommended her to Steven Spielberg for *The Color Purple*. It's a success secret that is available to anyone willing to use it.

## Employ Gradual Increase

Really solid long-lasting businesses are models of gradual increase. With every project or each month, set a goal to increase by five or ten percent. Do that consistently for a year and you'll see spectacular growth. Do that for a year and gradual increase will become a habitual way of growing your business. It's also a way to learn to enjoy the journey—not just the arrival. When you're truly passionate about what you're doing, even the disappointing times are better than doing something that steals your soul.

*To Affirm:* I am passionately committed to building my dreams.

*To Consider:* Discovered any effective ways to spend your down time? Have you ever had an experience where a greater opportunity came to you because you kept a commitment? What role does lukewarm commitment play in stories of failure?

# Out of Sync—And Loving It

*Many things have been achieved by those who chose not to leap into the mainstream.*
Joan Mondale

Last week I returned from a nearly perfect vacation. It began with three days in Las Vegas where we had a room at the breathtaking Bellagio hotel overlooking the fountains. There was also a Monet exhibit at the hotel which was stunning and another terrific exhibit at the Guggenheim Museum in the Venetian Hotel. It was a feast for the soul. July, of course, is off-season in this city where temperatures regularly top 100 degrees so crowds are almost nonexistent.

Off-season travel is just one of the perks of being self-employed. I do many things out of sync with the rest of the world. For instance, I never stand in line at the bank on Friday when wage earners are scrambling to deposit their paychecks. Stores are blissfully empty early in the morning so that's when I do my shopping. I can't remember the last time I stood in line to see a blockbuster movie; I prefer Tuesday afternoon matinees, which are almost like having a private screening. Not only is avoiding crowds less stressful, it's amazingly efficient. I can do errands in a fraction of the time it takes most people because I'm not doing so at busy times.

So what do I do with all that extra time? I spend lots of it on building my dreams, of course. And just recently, I've spent it reading some extraordinary things that I wanted to pass along to you this week.

## Contagious Kindness

This article from the *Washington Post* was a powerful reminder of how kindness can multiply. According to the story, a first-class passenger boarding a flight from Atlanta to Chicago noticed another passenger he apparently felt was more deserving of first-class treatment. "Hey, soldier, where are you sitting?" the first-class passenger asked. When the soldier returning from Iraq responded that he was assigned seat 22E, the first-class passenger said he wanted to change places with him.

That kind act had a domino effect and all the first-class passengers started giving soldiers their seats. There were 14 first-class seats but only 12 soldiers. One flight attendant cried and all were overwhelmed. "It put an entirely different mood on the entire flight."

## Elegant Gathering

I also finished an inspiring novel called *The Elegant Gathering of White Snows* by Kris Radish. It's the story of a group of women friends who spontaneously decide to walk away from their everyday lives. As they walk around the Wisconsin countryside, they each become clearer about changes they want to make in their own lives. Even more stunning is the impact their walk has on complete strangers who hear about them and are moved to act on their own abandoned dreams. It was a powerful reminder that when we follow our dreams, it can create a ripple effect we can't possibly imagine.

## Overcoming Resistance

Then there's Steven Pressfield's *The War of Art*, the most powerful book I've read in ages. In fact, I've been evangelizing about this one which is an insightful, funny and jolting look at the inner barriers we all have to success. Pressfield paints such a clear picture of resistance that it almost takes on physical form. Listen to this: "Resistance's goal is not to wound or disable. Resistance aims to kill. Its target is the epicenter of our being: our genius, our soul, the unique and priceless gift we were put on earth to give and that no one else has but us. Resistance means business. When we fight it, we are in a war to the death."

Fortunately, Pressfield arms his readers well, making it possible to get on with our important work and put resistance in its place. I love this book so much that I could stand on the street corner and pass it out. Anyone who's called me in the past few days has had to listen to me read favorite passages from it. Enough said. This belongs in your library. Now.

## Why This Matters

You know it as well as I do: to be a Dreambuilder in this world where conforming is a popular pastime is to be out of sync with the mainstream. Sometimes that can feel lonely. We might even question our sanity, wondering why we can't just settle for "good enough." But deep down we all know that good enough never is. "In this age," said John Stuart Mill, long ago, "the mere example of nonconformity, the mere refusal to bend the knee to custom, is itself a service." That's still true—and we're the ones to prove it.

*To Affirm:* I am comfortable being who I truly am.

*To Consider:* Besides empty movie theaters, what are some other rewards of being in charge of your own time? How can overcoming procrastination give us more time to use in satisfying ways? How can following our dreams create a domino effect?

# Silence Isn't Always Golden

*Courtesy is itself a form of service. By thoughtfulness for others in the little things we may smooth the roughness of life.*
Richard Dale

Shunning is a form of punishment still practiced in some religions. The wrongdoers may remain in the community but no one is allowed to speak to them. Shunning was also practiced in my family. After my parents and siblings moved to California while I was in college in Minnesota, I lived with an aunt for two years. She was a master at using the silent treatment to deal with my misbehavior. Besides the psychological pain that went with this behavior, silence is inherently ineffective since it doesn't address the real issue. Many times she would go for days without speaking to me while I remained clueless about what my offense had been.

Since I still have family members who resort to shunning when angered, I have had plenty of time to look at this harmful practice. I realized that the angry person thinks that the offense is so clear that the offender must certainly know they've behaved badly. But, of course, without clear communication, assumptions frequently prove false.

## Too Busy To Care?
Because of my years of enduring the silent treatment, you may think I'm a bit more sensitive to unanswered communication

than others are—but I don't believe that's the case. I'm an absolute stickler about responding as quickly as I can to telephone messages. In the majority of instances, the response is the same: "Oh, I didn't expect to hear from you so soon." I have to think that most people are used to waiting for days to have their calls returned.

If you're one of those people who are chronically too busy to respond quickly, I'd like you to consider the message that you're sending to your callers. This past year I've worked with two people who frequently go for days without responding to e-mails or voicemails. Now I am, in fact, their customer and they both know that I think fabulous service is one of the best products you can offer. So what's the deal? I became so frustrated with one of them that I left a message saying, "Do you treat all of your clients this way—or am I special?" Knowing how irritated I was (often because my business was interrupted while waiting for him to complete projects that were promised but not delivered on time), I feared for the future of his business if this was his standard operating method.

In all fairness, I have noticed that both of these tortoises are quick to apologize when they do finally get in touch. In both cases, the excuse is the same: we were busy. However, busyness isn't really as fine an alibi as they may think since the hidden message in that is, "I was taking care of my important customers ... and you aren't one of them."

## Avoiding Something?
Several months ago, Nick Williams and I were having a phone

chat and I told him I'd just spent a couple of days being cranky and that led me to retreat into my shell. "I didn't want to inflict myself on anyone else," I explained. He laughed and said, "So you were stuck being with your miserable self."

This is a real trap that we who are solo entrepreneurs can fall into. We're going through a rough patch, we lose a valuable client, we're stuck for a new idea, so we decide that the best way to avoid further rejection is to avoid everyone. Bad idea. Avoidance will only get us more of our misery. It's giving the silent treatment to whomever let us down—or to our own dreams.

Here's the kicker: communication is magic. Even if we can't go back to the client who quit on us or figure out what to do next on our own, talking to a trusted friend can put us back in the game quickly. Talking (not to be confused with perpetual whining) can break the spell and get anger or disappointment behind us.

### So Talk About It

Communication is tricky business. We see evidence of that everyday, but that's no reason to avoid it. Even amateur psychologists know that withholding communication can be a power trip. That's not a reputation you want to get. If you've procrastinated, if you aren't going to meet a deadline or if you think you've been misunderstood, keeping quiet isn't going to fix the problem. Speak up. Make it your ironclad policy to do what you say you're going to do—when you're going to do it. And if you can't keep your agreements, communicate that too.

The person you've let down might have a solution you haven't thought of. At the very least, they'll trust you more because you were honest. Whatever you do, shun shunning.

*To Affirm:* I make clear communication a high priority. I do what I say I'm going to do.

*To Consider:* Have you been the recipient of non-communication? How much frustration did it cause you? How do you feel when others make you a low priority? How conscious are you of showing appreciation and keeping people informed when necessary?

Nick Williams and I invite you to join our global network of inspired entrepreneurs. Go to www.dreambuilderscommunity.com to learn how. And while you're surfing the Internet, visit me at www.barbarawinter.com and Nick at www.heartatwork.com to learn about upcoming seminars, new products and resources.